Architectural Design Collaborators 3

Perlman/Stearns Inc.
80 Trowbridge Street, Cambridge/Massachusetts 02138

**Special thanks to the many people
whose support has been invaluable.**

Rita Perlman
Lori Perlman
Milton and Lanie Goldenberg
Larry and Sylvia Stearns
Kathy Furst
Nathan Furst

Mel Ingalls
Steven Trustman
Kevin Bottomley
Gardner McCormick

David Wasserman
Larry Schwartz
Bill Strong

Clifford Selbert Design

Lisa D'Ambrosio
DeFrancis Studio
Wendy Lurie
Theodore and Alice Thibodeau
Bill Harris
George Turnbull

Frank Costantino, ASAP
David Fraher, Arts Midwest
Elizabeth Goodrich, IDSA
Marion Greene, IALD
Lynn Learned, BCG
Jacquie Schiewe, IBD
Sarah Speare, SEGD
Richard Weisgrau, ASMP

Credits

Publisher/President	**Robert W. Perlman**
Vice-President, Marketing/Sales	**Arthur Furst**
Marketing/Sales Staff	**James Edwards** **Brian McCarron** **Christopher Burbul**
Systems Coordinator	**Ted Thibodeau, Jr.**
Marketing/Production Assistant	**M. Noel Page**
Production Manager	**Denise Kissel**
Graphic Design Consultant	**D.K. Design**
Copy/Layout Editor	**Melinda Baker**
Cover Photo	**James Edwards**
Printing/Color Separations	**Toppan Printing Co.** **(America)**
Distributed exclusively worldwide by	**Rockport Publishers, Inc.** P.O. Box 396 5 Smith Street Rockport/Massachusetts 01966 Telephone: (508) 546-9590 Fax: (508) 546-7141 Telex: 5106019284 ROCKORT PUB

Printed in Singapore

The A/DC staff is comprised of professionals in
marketing, photography, illustration and graphic
design. This balance of skills exemplifies the firm's
commitment to the spirit of collaboration. In that spirit,
A/DC encourages design professionals and industry
organizations to contact the firm and share ideas on
further enhancing communications among the design
professions. For more information on participation in
A/DC, call 617.497.1213.

ISBN# 0-9624219-4-4

■ Illustrators/Renderers

American Society of Architectural Perspectivists Information

Alphabetical Listing

IR

American Society of Architectural Perspectivists

National Office c/o:

Boston Architectural Center
320 Newbury Street
Boston, MA 02115

617.846.4766

Philosophy and Purpose

The American Society of Architectural Perspectivists (ASAP) was founded in 1986 as a representative organization to foster communication among architectural perspectivists, to raise the standards of design drawing and illustration worldwide, and to acquaint a broader public with the importance of such drawing as an adjunct to architectural design.

ASAP believes that by recognizing, celebrating, and disseminating the highest achievements in architectural drawing and painting, the quality of the work - and the working - will be heightened. With more sensitive, more accurate, and more professional architectural drawing, ASAP believes that architecture itself will be enhanced, resulting in benefit for all.

Membership

Membership is open to professional illustrators, architects, designers, students, and anyone engaged in the serious pursuit of drawing as a design and presentation tool in architecture. Overseas professional membership is available to international practitioners.

To encourage greater participatory opportunities for members and aspiring practitioners, active regional chapters are located in Chicago, Toronto, Seattle, Atlanta, San Francisco and Dallas. Advisory coordinators may be contacted in New York, Detroit, Philadelphia, St. Louis, San Jose and Calgary, Canada. International coordinators from seven foreign countries serve as liaison to a growing overseas membership. Prospective members can request an informational booklet, with application, from the Society's headquarters.

Activities and Awards

The Society sponsors an annual competitive exhibition and convention, which brings together the best current works and practitioners of architectural drawing from the United States, Canada and around the world. Since their inception, ASAP's exhibits have been on view in major cities throughout the US as well as feature displays of AIA national conventions. The works are selected from submissions by a jury of respected professionals from the fields of architecture, illustration, and design education. The drawing judged to be the year's best of show may be accorded the highest award of the Society, the Hugh Ferriss Memorial Prize. ASAP, with funding from the Van Nostrand Reinhold Company, has established this award for excellence in the graphic representation of architecture. The Ferriss Prize is an award of a specially cast medallion, presented to the winner at the Society's convention.

Publications

ASAP publishes *Architecture in Perspective*, an annual catalogue featuring the selected work of each year's exhibition. Distributed by ASAP and VNR through bookstores, universities and mail order, the catalogue contains information on each artist and his/her respective drawing. Each of the four editions still available (1988 AIP III – 1991 AIP VI) serves as an invaluable reference source of services for the architectural and related professions. The catalogue is effective at broadening the exposure and increasing the geographic market base of many member exhibitors.

Architecture in Perspective: A Five-Year Retrospective of Award-Winning Illustration, published by Van Nostrand Reinhold, is a hardcover book compilation of the exhibition catalogues and is available in most bookstores.

The Society provides a quarterly newsletter, *Convergence*, an attorney-designed standardized delineator's contract, and a national membership roster to its members. Transcripts of seminars on business practice and drawing issues are also available.

Special Programs

ASAP in conjunction with AIA, serves as a national clearing house and referral agency for architects and developers seeking the services of perspectivists. The Society sustains substantial worldwide communications with foreign affiliate organizations, i.e., the British Society of Architectural Illustrators and the Japan Architectural Renderers Association. Periodic contact is also maintained with the Australian, Chinese, Korean, German, Irish and other Asian and European rendering communities. Regular international exchange of drawings, slides and publications expands the scope of the illustrators concerns and develops an understanding of foreign practitioners' work.

The Society annually sponsors seminars, workshops and lectures on a wide range of illustration techniques and business practices, both to its members and the architectural community. These are offered in conjunction with ASAP's and AIA's convention and at the various venues of our exhibit, *Architecture in Perspective*. ASAP likewise provides current information on legal issues and marketing practices.

TABLE OF CONTENTS

William Gary Mellenbruch

Mellenbruch Studio Inc.
8118 NW Forest Drive
Kansas City / Missouri
64152

816.587.9565
800.345.DRAW Toll Free
816.587.2887 Fax

Selected Projects

3. Embassy Suites Hotel
Sarasota, FL
Developer:
**John Q. Hammons
Industries**
Architect:
Steve Minton
Springfield, MO

4. Galleria Complex
Tulsa, OK
Architect:
Architects Collective
Tulsa, OK

Architectural Clients Include

**Nearing, Staats,
Preloger & Jones**
Shawnee Mission, KS

Hansen, Lind, Meyer
Iowa City, IA

**Helmuth, Obata &
Kassabaum**
Kansas City, MO

Page Sutherland Page
Austin, TX

**How Nelson &
Associates**
Omaha, NE

Sherlock Smith & Adams
Montgomery, AL

William Graves
Pensacola, FL

Vitols Associates
Boston

Environmental Design
Des Moines, IA

A.W. Nelson
Pine Bluff, AR

A.G. Spanos
Las Vegas, NV

J.C. Nichols Company
Kansas City, MO

Paragon Group
St. Louis, MO

■ Bruce Mayron

Bruce Mayron, BFA
Architectural Renderings
201 West 21st Street
Suite 15D
New York / New York
10011

212.633.1503

Mixing the best of perspectives drawn to scale with the trained eye of a fine artist.

Able to work within any budget. Fast turn around without sacrifice of quality.

Wide variety of styles available to accommodate any need. Very sensitive to illustrating the subtle qualities of each project.

Creates renderings - from plans or inspirational photographs - that will effectively sell the project.

Degree: Bachelor of Fine Arts Cum Laude in Interior Design, The Maryland Institute College of Art. Additional studies completed at the Art Students League of New York.

Clients Include

Reebok, Inc.

Helmsley Palace Hotel
(New York City)

Ponderosa Steakhouses

Metromedia

B.B. King

Barbie Doll International
(a division of Mattel Toys)

Hardy, Holzman, Pfeiffer

■ Michael McCann

Michael McCann
Associates, Ltd.
2 Gibson Avenue
Toronto / Ontario
Canada
M5R 1T5

416.964.7532
416.964.2060 Fax

An architectural rendering company specializing in watercolor perspectives for an exclusive worldwide clientele.

Founded in 1971.

Selected Projects

Euro-Disney
Paris
Architect:
Skidmore, Owings & Merrill
New York City

Tokyo Forum Competition
Tokyo
Architect:
James Sterling Michael Wilford & Associates
London

Metropolitan Life Building
North Project
New York City
Architect:
Kohn Pedersen Fox Conway
New York City

Jeddah Airport
Competition
Jeddah, Saudi Arabia
Architect:
Skidmore, Owings & Merrill
Chicago

Disney Studios
Anaheim, CA
Architect:
Cooper/Robertson & Partners
New York City

Portcullis Competition
London
Architect:
Zeidler / Roberts Partnership
Toronto
London

■ Lee Dunnette

Lee Dunnette
21 Stuyvesant Oval
Suite 2E
New York / New York
10009

212.260.4240

Techniques

Ink rendering with
transparent color

Ink line drawing with
transparent airbrush color

Full-color opaque acrylic

Color acrylic
photomontage

Black Prismacolor pencil

**Architectural Clients
Include**

**Pei Cobb Freed &
Partners**
New York City

**Kohn Pederson Fox
Associates**
New York City

Hardy Holzman Pfieffer
New York City

Fox & Fowle Architects
New York City

**Hellmuth Obata
Kassabaum**
New York City

**Rafael Vinoly &
Associates**
New York City

**Cooper Robertson &
Partners**
New York City

Beyer Blinder Belle
New York City

**Costas Kondylis
Architects**
New York City

**Ehrenkrantz Eckstut &
Whitelaw**
New York City

■ Edward Dumont

Edward Dumont
1461 Pueblo Drive
Pittsburgh / Pennsylvania
15228

412.343.2544

Techniques

Felt tip and line
conceptuals for all areas
of design

Pen and ink

Watercolor washes
and glazes

Airbrush

Pastel

Prismacolor pencils

Matting and framing
for presentation

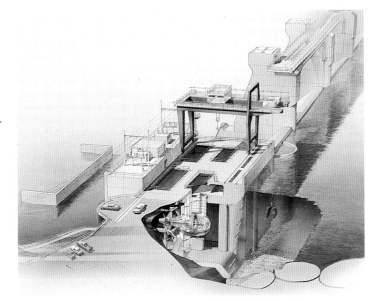

Architectural Clients Include

Bechtel National Inc.
New Martinsville, WV

Oxford Development , Inc.
Pittsburgh, PA

Williams / Trebilcock / Whitehead
Pittsburgh, PA

Bonita Bay Properties, Inc.
Bonita Springs, FL

L. Robert Kimball Associates
Edensburg, PA

Tasso Katselas Associates
Pittsburgh, PA

The Design Alliance
Pittsburgh, PA

IKM Incorporated
Pittsburgh, PA

GWSM Landscape Architects
Pittsburgh, PA

■ PRELIM, Inc.

PRELIM, Inc.
Robert Cook, President
8330 Medow Road #210
Dallas / Texas
75231

214.692.7226
800.541.0492 Toll Free
214.692.7286 Fax

Techniques

Edge to edge tempera

Vignettes

Special effects
(night scenes)

Pen and ink

Pen, ink, and watercolor

Photo montage

Computer-generated
perspectives

Selected Projects

1. JC Penny Corporate
Headquarters
Plano, TX
Architect:
HKS Architects
Dallas

2. Renaissance Center
Bridgeport, CT
Architect:
**Architects
Environmental
Collaborative**
New Haven, CT

3. JC Penny Corporate
Headquarters
Plano, TX
Architect:
HKS Architects
Dallas

2

3

Offering a selection of
the most beautiful and
innovative approaches in
the field of architectural
presentation. Known for
flexibility and architectural
precision, with a growing
national and worldwide
reputation for excellence.
Color brochure available.

■ Blackman Architectural Illustrators

Blackman Architectural
Illustrators, Inc.
150 SW 12th Avenue
Suite 310
Pompano Beach / Florida
33069

305.781.5302
305.781.5303 Fax

Techniques

Broadline Pencil

Pen & Ink

Felt-tip / Marker

Watercolor

Airbrush

A quarter of a century of accomplishments creating dramatic and appealing residential, commercial, and industrial architectural renderings. Proven success in both interior and exterior work, as well as hand and computer-generated designs.

A nation-wide reputation for exceptional quality and fast service within the client's budget and time constraints.

Projects successfully completed for architects, engineers, developers, interior designers, and industrial designers.

Fax and modem equipment allow for quick approvals and world-wide access.

Services

Presentations

Displays

■ Art Associates, Inc.

Art Associates, Inc.
4635 West Alexis Road
Toledo / Ohio
43623-1005

419.537.1303
419.474.9113 Fax

Services

Illustrations in any style

Advertising design and art

In-house photography and printing

Graphic arts, films, stats, veloxes, typesetting, and lithography

Computer animation, video imaging, and scanning, from wire frames to fully rendered images

Architectural, engineering, topographic, and product prototype models.

Desk reference with 185 color plates available on request.

Providing architects, engineers, developers, and advertising agencies worldwide with over 20,000 commissions since 1966.

■ Art Associates, Inc.

Art Associates, Inc.
4635 West Alexis Road
Toledo / Ohio
43623-1005

419.537.1303
419.474.9113 Fax

5

6

Selected Projects

1. Gran Central Center
Miami
Architect:
**Smallwood, Reynolds,
Stewart & Stewart**
Atlanta

2. Universal Studios
Theme Park
Orlando, FL
Client:
Universal Studios
Orlando, FL

3. Nationwide Insurance
World Headquarters
Columbus, OH
Architect:
BOHM NBBJ
Columbus, OH

4. Clemson University
Stadium
Client:
Graphics Plus
Greenville, SC

5. Church Interior
(photo retouch - area
between pews and light
fixtures is all painted in)
Architect:
Weibel Rudzewski
Erie, PA

6. Chase Retreat
Belize
Client:
Mars Advertising
Detroit, MI

■ Tainer Associates, Ltd.

Tainer Associates, Ltd.
213 West Institute Place
Suite 301
Chicago / Illinois
60610

312.951.1656
312.951.8773 Fax

Clients Include

RREEF Funds

Stein & Company

L.J. Sheridan & Company

JMB Realty

The John Buck Company

Tishman Speyer
Properties

The Hoffman Group

Tanguay Burke & Stratton

Diversified Capital
Group, Inc.

Pulte Home Corporation

United Development
Company, Inc.

Balcor Development
Company

The Prime Group

Limpro, Inc.

Rubloff, Inc.

Draper & Kramer, Inc.

**Architectural Clients
Include**

**Skidmore, Owings &
Merrill**
Chicago

Lohan Associates
Chicago

Perkins & Will
Chicago

VOA Associates
Chicago

ISD, Inc.
Chicago

Powell / Kleinschmidt
Chicago

**Pappageorge /
Haymes Ltd.**
Chicago

The Landahl Group
Chicago

**Hague Richards
Associates**
Chicago

**Swanke Hayden
Connell Architects**
Chicago

HOK
St. Louis

**Camburas &
Theodore, Inc.**
Chicago

Horn & Associates
Chicago

Multi-disciplined design
studio offering a full
range of ink, marker, air
brush, and mixed media
illustrations.

Language Fluency: Italian,
French, and Spanish

■ James Edwards, Illustration

James Edwards
Sherman Street Studios
7 Sherman Street
Boston / Massachusetts
02129

617.522.2656
617.241.8344

Selected Project

Clocktower Place
Nashua, NH

Illustrations conveying the beauty, historic quality, and commercial potential of Nashua's newly renovated mill buildings.

Commissioned by the developer for use in a full color brochure and other sales materials.

Framed originals also showcased in the developer's on-site offices as sales tools for client viewing during the renovation and construction phases.

Specializing in fine architectural watercolors for renovation and historical projects, incorporating lifelike human characters as they relate to specified environments.

Realistic treatment of the planned landscape and foliage in a traditional style and technique complements the technical accuracy of the architectural details.

Also experienced in illustrations for publication in marketing, advertising, and editorial materials.

■ Richard Rochon

Rochon Associates, Inc.
13530 Michigan Avenue
Suite 205
Dearborn / Michigan
48126

313.584.9580
313.584.4071 Fax

Advisory Council:
American Society of
Architectural Perspectivists

Member: New York
Society of Renderers

Author: *Color in
Architectural Illustration*
(Van Nostrand Reinhold
1989)

Honorary Member:
Michigan Society of
Architects

1

■ Richard Rochon

Rochon Associates, Inc.
13530 Michigan Avenue
Suite 205
Dearborn / Michigan
48126

313.584.9580
313.584.4071 Fax

Architectural Clients
Include

1. **Skidmore, Owings &
Merrill**
New York City

2. **Rossetti Associates**
Detroit

Arquitectonica
Coral Gables, FL
Chicago

**Cambridge Seven
Associates**
Cambridge, MA

Ellerbe Becket
Washington, DC

**Hellmuth Obata
Kassabaum**
New York City
Washington, DC

James Stewart Polshek
New York City

**Skidmore, Owings &
Merrill**
Chicago

**Smith, Hinchman &
Grylls**
Detroit

**Minoru Yamasaki &
Associates**
Troy, MI

2

■ Frank Bartus

Genesis Studios
One Gateway Center
Suite 501
Newton / Massachusetts
02158

800 N. Magnolia Avenue
Suite 1201
Orlando / Florida
32803

800.933.9380 Toll Free

Architectural Clients Include

RTKL
Baltimore

Odell Associates
Charlotte, NC

Reynolds, Smith & Hills
Tampa, FL

Hammel, Green & Abrahamson
Minneapolis, MN

Walt Disney World Design & Engineering
Orlando

The Architects Collaborative
Cambridge, MA

Selected Projects

1. Sandy Lake Towers
Orlando, FL
Architect:
The Scott Companies
Orlando, FL

2. McCormick Place
Chicago
Architect:
VOA & Associates
Chicago

Brochures available on request.

■ Frank Bartus

Genesis Studios
One Gateway Center
Suite 501
Newton / Massachusetts
02158

800 N. Magnolia Avenue
Suite 1201
Orlando / Florida
32803

800.933.9380 Toll Free

Experienced illustrator dedicated to the artistic expression of architecture. Working for 20 years with America's foremost studios, including futurist painter Syd Mead. Specializes in full color exterior perspectives, combining the precision of architecture with the artist's flair to subtly reflect the nuances of a specific design setting.

Attention to schedule and budgetary requirements assures a pleasant and productive working relationship.

Selected Projects

3. Library Building
South Florida
Community College
Architect:
VOA Architects
Orlando, FL

4. Guam Legislature
Building
Architect:
**Beckhard Richlan
Arizala Joint Venture
Architects**
New York City

3

4

■ James C. Smith

The Studio of
James C. Smith
700 South Clinton Street
Chicago / Illinois
60607

312.987.0132
312.987.0099 Fax

Clients Include

DeStefano / Goettsch

Murphy / Jahn

Perkins & Will

Skidmore, Owings &
Merrill
(Chicago &
Washington DC)

Trammell Crow Company

DePaul University

City of Chicago

Art Institute of Chicago

Selected Project

The Rookery Building
Chicago
Developer:
**Baldwin Development
Company**
Chicago

Creating a serene sense
of design and pattern
while illustrating
architectural treatments,
this painting depicts the
restoration of the oriel
stairway and light court
of the Burnham & Root's
Rookery Building. It is one
of seven images that
detailed the restoration
concepts. The view was
constructed with
traditional methods and
shows the stained glass
with ornamental iron
patterns, various metal
components of the stair,
and the outer wall
assembly.

Techniques

Line & color illustrations

Airbrush paintings

Photographic retouching

Trompe l'oeil mural
painting

■ Lori Brown

Lori Brown
Consultants Ltd.
1639 West 2nd Avenue
Vancouver / British
Columbia
Canada
V6J 1H3

604.685.0401 Office
604.224.4035 Home
604.685.2795 Fax

Architectural illustration
in mixed media ranging
from loose concept
sketches to final
presentation drawings.

Selected Projects

1. Residential Project
Vancouver, BC
Architect:
**Hancock Nicolson
Tamaki**
Vancouver, BC

2. Capilano College Library
N. Vancouver, BC
Architect:
Henriquez & Partners
Vancouver, BC

Expo '92
Seville, Spain
Concept Design &
Illustration

Expo '86
Vancouver, BC
Color Program &
Illustration

"Pearls of Kuwait"
Competition
Kuwait City, Kuwait
Architect:
**Arthur Erickson
Associates**
Vancouver, BC

1

2

Member: American
Association of
Architectural
Perspectivists

■ Dan Harmon

Dan Harmon & Associates
2839 Paces Ferry Road
Suite 370
Atlanta / Georgia
30339

404.436.0854
404.333.8970 Fax

**Architectural Clients
Include**

**John Portman &
Associates**
Atlanta

**Thompson, Ventulett &
Stainback**
Atlanta

Cousins Properties, Inc.
Atlanta

Gerald Hines Interests
Atlanta

Carter & Associates
Atlanta

**Interstate Hotels
Corporation**
Pittsburgh, PA

Marriott Corporation
Lakeland, FL

HOK
New York City

Odell Associates
Charlotte, NC

Awards

The American Society of
Architectural Perspectivists
1988, 1990

American Institute of
Architects (Atlanta
Chapter)
Service to the Profession
1980, 1989

■ David A. Anderson

David A. Anderson
Architectural Illustration
PO Box 7055
1316 Chestnut Street
San Carlos / California
94070-4715

415.592.1868

Specializing in exterior
and interior acrylic
renderings for architects,
engineers, and developers.
Other presentation media
include pencil, pen and
ink, and pen and ink with
watercolor.

Member: American
Society of Architectural
Perspectivists

**Architectural Clients
Include**

**Design & Engineering
Systems, Inc.**
Redwood City, CA

**Leo A. Daly &
Associates**
San Francisco

Ehrlich • Rominger
San Francisco
Los Altos, CA

**Gensler & Associates
Architects**
San Francisco

GHI Architects
San Francisco

**Hornberger Worstell &
Associates**
San Francisco

**Kaplan • McLaughlin •
Diaz**
San Francisco

**McLellan &
Copenhagen, Inc.**
Cupertino, CA

**Bent Severin &
Associates**
San Francisco

**Orlando Diaz-Azcuy
Designs**
San Francisco

Selected Project

600 California Street
San Francisco
Architect:
**Kohn Pederson Fox
Associates**
New York City

■ Frank Costantino

F.M. Costantino, Inc.
13b Pauline Street
Winthrop / Massachusetts
02152

617.846.4766
617.846.4766 Fax

Selected Project

New Tanglewood Concert
Hall (summer home of the
Boston Symphony
Orchestra)
Lenox, MA
Architect:
**William Rawn &
Associates**
Boston

Delineation in the
tradition of fine
architectural drawing,
providing the discerning
client with distinctive
illustrations of
architecture.

Co-founder: American
Society of Architectural
Perspectivists

Fellow: Society of
Architectural Illustrators
(Great Britain)

Honorary Member: Japan
Architectural Renderers
Association

Please refer to A/DC 1
and 2 for further examples
of work.

■ Frank Costantino

F.M. Costantino, Inc.
13b Pauline Street
Winthrop / Massachusetts
02152

617.846.4766
617.846.4766 Fax

Publications

Architecture in Perspective: A Five-Year Retrospective of Award-Winning Illustration
(Van Nostrand Reinhold 1991)

Architectural Rendering
(Quarto Publishing Ltd. 1991)

Architectural Delineation: A Photographic Approach to Presentation
(McGraw Hill 1991)

Selected Project

Maxwell School
Syracuse University
Syracuse, NY
Architect:
Bohlin, Cywinkski, Jackson
Wilkes-Barre, PA

■ Gregory Cloud

Gregory Cloud Associates
2116 Arlington Avenue
Suite 236
Los Angeles / California
90018

213.484.9479
213.734.0515 Fax

**Architectural Clients
Include**

RTKL Associates
Los Angeles

Altoon & Porter
Los Angeles

Jerde Partnership, Ltd.
Los Angeles

**Walt Disney
Imagineering**
Los Angeles

AC Martin
Los Angeles

SDI
Los Angeles

**DeBretteville &
Polyzoides**
Los Angeles

**Steven Ehrlich
Associates**
Venice, CA

**Richard Magee &
Associates**
Los Angeles

**Johannes Van Tilburg
& Partners**
Los Angeles

Other Clients Include

Ahmanson Development

Maguire Thomas Partners

MCA Universal

Treptow Development

Caldwell Banker, REIBS

Dames & Moore

Robert Englekirk

JMB Realty

Chandler Group

The Ratkovich Company

Providing architects and
developers with
personalized service and
high quality illustrations
using traditional and
digital techniques.

Services include
presentation graphics, 3D
computer animation, and
photo services.

■ Thomas Demko

Thomas Demko
326 Maple Avenue
Pittsburgh / Pennsylvania
15218

412.242.3721

Selected Project

Carrie Furnaces
Pittsburgh, PA
study sketches
Architect:
**Landmarks Design
Associates**
Pittsburgh, PA

Offering a traveling
rendering service for quick
in-office sketches or
conceptual studies.

Works executed in pen
and ink line, watercolor,
marker, or acrylic.

■ Tamotsu Yamamoto

Yamamoto Architectural
Illustration
15 Sleeper Street
Boston / Massachusetts
02210

617.542.1021
617.451.0271 Fax

Services include watercolor,
gouache, pen and ink,
airbrush, other drawing
media, and computer-
generated perspectives.

Able to work with architect
or developer in early stages
of design conceptualization,
creating quick sketches in
any medium through final
presentation drawings.

Instructor in architectural
perspectives and
illustration since 1979 at
institutions including the
Massachusetts College of
Art and the Boston
Architectural Center.

Member/Officer: American
Society of Architectural
Perspectivists

Member: Japan
Architectural Renderers
Association

**Architectural Clients
Include**

**The Architects
Collaborative**
Cambridge, MA

**Architectural Resources
Cambridge, Inc.**
Cambridge, MA

Carlson Associates, Inc.
Cochituate, MA

**Elkus Manfredi
Architects, Ltd.**
Boston

LEA Group, Inc.
Boston

**Todd Lee Clark Rozas
Associates, Inc.**
Boston

**Nikken Sekkei
International, Inc.**
New York City

Tufts University
Medford, MA

**Daniel F. Tully
Associates, Inc.**
Melrose, MA

Selected Projects

1. Tufts University
Dormitory
Medford, MA
using watercolor as a
final presentation medium
Architect:
**Architectural Resources
Cambridge, Inc.**
Cambridge, MA

2, 3.Examples of 24-hour
service, using a technique
that combines both
watercolor and tempera.

Charlie Manus

Architectural
Presentation Arts
43 Union Avenue #1
Memphis / Tennessee
38103

901.525.4335
901.527.1143 Fax

Selected Projects

1. City of Memphis Trolley
Project
Memphis, TN
Architect:
Hnedak, Bobo Group
Memphis, TN

2. Hampton Inn
Boston
Architect:
Looney, Ricks, Kiss
Memphis, TN

3. Purchasing Facility
Sarasota County School
Board
Sarasota, FL
Architect:
**George Palermo &
Associates**
Sarasota, FL

Clients Include

ADG

Federal Express

Holiday Corporation

Plough Inc.

RCA Cylix

Vantage Companies

Trammell Crow

Weston Companies

Belz Enterprises

Richards Medical

Promus

JMGR

D. E. Miller &
Associates

Hood-Rich

Forcum-Lannom, Inc.

Johnson Properties

Pyramid Companies

1

2

3

Twenty-four years of
providing high-quality
renderings. Techniques
include pencil, pen and
ink, colored acetate, and
air brush for site plans,
elevations, vignettes, and
full color renderings.

■ Richard Sneary

Sneary Architectural
Illustration
323 West Eighth Street
Kansas City / Missouri
64105

816.421.7771
800.886.7117

Publications

Architectural Record

Progressive Architecture

*Architectural Rendering
Techniques*
Mike Lin
(Van Nostrand, 1985)

*Architectural Drawing:
Options for Design*
Paul Lasseau
(Design Press, 1991)

1

Member: American
Institute of Architects;
American Society of
Architectural Perspectivists

■ Richard Sneary

Sneary Architectural
Illustration
323 West Eighth Street
Kansas City / Missouri
64105

816.421.7771
800.886.7117

2

Selected Project

1. Exterior View
2. Atrium Interior
LaSalle Plaza
Minneapolis, MN
Client:
Beta West Properties
Minneapolis, MN
Architect:
Ellerbe Becket
Minneapolis, MN

Exhibitions

*Architecture in Perspective
IV, V, & VI*
Traveling Exhibition
1989, 1990, & 1991

Art by Architects
Bedyk Gallery
Kansas City
1984

■ Markus Lui

Doug Chun & Associates
450 Mission Street
Suite 508
San Francisco / California
94105

415.541.4946
510.523.7640

Offering architectural
renderings with exterior,
interior, or aerial view.
Conceptual sketches and
quick executions also
available.

**Architectural Clients
Include**

Bechtel Corporation
San Francisco

SWA Group
Laguna Beach, CA

Tectonics
San Francisco
San Diego

Kaplan.McLaughlin.Diaz
San Francisco

**George Miers &
Associates**
San Francisco

**Eugene Lew &
Associates**
San Francisco

Techniques

Pencil

Pen & Ink

Watercolor

Tempera

Photo Montage

■ Sam Ringman

Ringman Design &
Illustration
2700 Fairmount
Suite 100
Dallas / Texas
75201

214.871.9001

Exhibitions

Annual Awards Exhibitions
American Society
of Architectural
Perspectivists
Chicago 1989
Boston 1990
New York City 1991

Architectural Clients Include

Hellmuth, Obata & Kassabaum
Dallas
London

Trammell Crow Company
Dallas
Los Angeles

Harwood K. Smith & Partners
Dallas

Corgan Associates Architects
Dallas

Omniplan
Dallas

Hermanovski Lauck Design
Dallas

Healthcare Environment Design
Dallas

Interprise / Southwest
Dallas

Herman Miller
Dallas

RTKL Associates
Dallas

Registered architect
producing architectural
and interior renderings in
a variety of media,
including pen and ink,
pencil, colored pencil,
marker, and water color.

■ Rael D. Slutsky

Rael D. Slutsky &
Associates, Inc.
8 South Michigan Avenue
Suite 310
Chicago / Illinois
60603

312.580.1995
312.580.1980 Fax

A creative and
professional source for
the finest architectural
renderings. Staff of
architect-artists has
serviced an international
clientele for more than 14
years.

Drawing techniques range
from quick freehand
design sketches to formal,
detailed pen and ink
renderings. The process
yields both black and
white and color originals
of each image. Portfolio
furnished upon request.

Advisory Council
Chairman and Executive
Board Member: American
Society of Architectural
Perspectivists.

Member: American
Institute of Architects

Exhibitions

American Society of
Architectural
Perspectivists Annual
Awards Exhibition
1987, 1988, 1989, 1991

Japanese Architectural
Renderers Association
Annual Exhibition
Tokyo 1989, 1990

■ Rael D. Slutsky

Rael D. Slutsky &
Associates, Inc.
8 South Michigan Avenue
Suite 310
Chicago / Illinois
60603

312.580.1995
312.580.1980 Fax

**Architectural Clients
Include**

**Skidmore Owings &
Merrill**
(nationwide)

**Cesar Pelli &
Associates**
New Haven, CT

**Hellmuth, Obata &
Kassabaum**
St. Louis
New York City

**Kevin Roche John
Dinkeloo & Associates**
Hamden, CT

Murphy / Jahn
Chicago

Perkins & Will
Chicago

Holabird & Root
Chicago

Odell & Associates, Inc.
Charlotte, NC

Altoon & Porter
Los Angeles

**Pei Cobb Freed &
Partners**
New York City

Cooper Cary
Atlanta

RTKL
Dallas

Kunwon International
Seoul, Korea

Il Sin Architects
Seoul, Korea

■ Florence S. Nahikian

Florence S. Nahikian
286 Hackett Hill Road
Hooksett /
New Hampshire
03106

603.641.6418
603.645.6661 Fax

Practicing architectural communication since 1976 for an international clientele of architectural, interior design, landscaping, and development firms in the US, France, and the Middle East.

Expression techniques range from fluid conceptual sketches to formal , crisp renderings and complete presentations in a variety of media, such as pen and ink, graphite, color pencil, pastel, color marker, gouache, and watercolor.

Clients Include

A Wogenski (France)

Berthet-Godet (France)

P. Y. Taralon (France)

Schemes (Saudi Arabia)

Carur Inc.(Lebanon)

Seven Up (Nigeria)

Batimark Inc. (Canada)

Newstress International

Norwood Realty

Hoyle, Tanner & Associates

Howard Johnson

Epoch Corporation

NYNEX

Sunoco

Honda

Stein Consultants

Member: American Society of Architectural Perspectivists

Degree: Master of Interior Architecture

■ Eric Schleef

Eric Schleef Illustration
7740 Dean Road
Indianapolis / Indiana
46240

317.595.0016
317.595.0016 Fax

Specializing in versatile
line and mixed-media
color illustration. Quick
sketches, pencil, and
watercolor techniques
are also available. Able
to work from conceptual
sketches and working
drawings, at the studio
or on location with the
design team.

Member: American
Society of Architectural
Perspectivists

**Architectural Clients
Include**

**Browning Day
Mullins Dierdorf**
Indianapolis

**Group Eleven
Architecture &
Planning**
Indianapolis

**Howard Needles
Tammen & Bergendoff**
Indianapolis

Kasler & Associates
Cincinnati

**The Odle McGuire &
Shook Corporation**
Indianapolis

**Schmidt Associates
Architects**
Indianapolis

**Swanke Hayden
Connell Architects**
Chicago

**Tomblinson Harburn
Associates**
Flint, MI

Other Clients Include

Eli Lilly & Company

Kiwanis Magazine

Earlham College

Shuel Advertising

The National Art
Museum of Sport

Richard C. Baehr

Richard C. Baehr, AIA
Architectural Rendering
305 Northern Boulevard
Great Neck / New York
11021

516.466.0470
516.466.1670 Fax

Selected Projects

1. The Court at One
International Place
Boston
Architect:
John Burgee Architects
New York City

2. Retail Arcade
The Bond Building
Sydney, Australia
Architect:
Kohn Pederson Fox
New York City

3. St. Charles Cemetery
Mausoleum
Long Island, NY
Architect:
**Angelo Francis Corva
& Associates**
Uniondale, NY

4. 270 Madison Avenue
Renovation
New York City
Architect:
**Max Gordon &
Associates**

1

2

Specializing in full-color
tempera renderings. Other
media include pencil on
mylar, pen and ink, and
photo montage.

Member: American
Institute of Architects;
American Society of
Architectural Perspectivists

■ Richard C. Baehr

Richard C. Baehr, AIA
Architectural Rendering
305 Northern Boulevard
Great Neck / New York
11021

516.466.0470
516.466.1670 Fax

3

4

**Architectural Clients
Include**

Ammann & Whitney
New York City

Edward Larrabee Barnes
New York City

John Burgee Architects
New York City

**Castro Blanco Piscioneri
& Associates**
New York City

**Angelo Francis Corva &
Associates**
Uniondale, NY

Davis, Brody Associates
New York City

**Costas Kondylis
Architects**
New York City

Mojo Stumer Architects
Roslyn Heights, NY

**Cesar Pelli &
Associates**
New Haven, CT

Der Scutt Architect
New York City

Other Clients Include

Bellemead Development
Corporation

Brookhaven National
Laboratory

Gerald D. Hines Interests

The Trump Organization

Richard Zirinsky Associates

■ T. Lynn Craven

Architectural Images, Inc.
501 W Peachtree Street
Lakeland / Florida
33801-1534

813.687.4946
813.688.4847 Fax

President of Architectural Images, Inc., a full service architectural firm, and of Northface Corporation Inc., a computer graphics and architectural animation company.

Success is based on quality presentation, assuring project success.

21 years experience in architectural and technical illustration, pen & ink, ink with marker, watercolor, pencil/prisma color, air brush, pastel, computer paste-up, and architectural animation.

Member: American Institute of Architects; American Society of Architectural Perspectivists

Clients Include

Lakeland Downtown Development

Lenox Properties

Warnock Properties

M & M Properties

Herring Management

Hauger-Bunch Inc.

Enco Development Inc.

Florida Centers Inc.

Clyde Parlier, AIA

Land Advertising

Thoroughbred Advertising

Harcourt, Brace, Jovanovich

L. Luria & Son Inc.

Publix Supermarkets

■ Gordon Grice

Gordon Grice & Associates
878 Queen Street West
Toronto, Ontario, Canada
M6J 1G3

416.536.9191
416.538.9413

Freehand pen and ink illustration; with or without coloured pencil toning. Accurate and/or fanciful. 17 years of rendering experience.

Member: Royal Architectural Institute of Canada, Ontario Association of Architects, Toronto Society of Architects

President: American Society of Architectural Perspectivists

Exhibitions

American Society of Architectural Perspectivists Juried Exhibitions, 1989, 1991

Japanese Architectural Renderers Association, 10th Anniversary Exhibition Tokyo, Japan, 1990

Ontario Association of Architects Invitational Exhibit, Toronto, 1991

Selected Project

Deerhurst Highlands
Huntsville, ON (Canada)
Architects:
**Zeidler Roberts
Partnership**
Toronto
Client:
**Deerhurst Resorts
Limited**
Huntsville, ON (Canada)

■ Barry N. Nathan

Barry R. Nathan
2666 East Bayshore Road
Palo Alto / California
94303

415.424.0980
415.856.3266 Fax

Selected Project

Proposed Hotel Casino
Queensland, Australia
Architect:
Robert Sprague
San Francisco

Architectural exterior and
interior renderings in a
variety of media and
techniques, from loose
pencil sketches to finished
airbrush. 3D CAD
capability.

Registered Architect

Member: American
Association of Architectural
Perspectivists

■ Barbara Morello

Morello Design Studios, Inc.
7 Jackes Avenue
Suite 1105
Toronto / Ontario
Canada
M4T 1E3

416.963.4315

Tacoma / Washington
206.572.6106

Specializing in watercolour interior and exterior architectural perspectives.

Architectural Clients Include

Carlos Ott
Toronto

Norr
Toronto

Housden Barnard
Los Angeles

Ziedler Roberts
Toronto

Barton Gillet
Baltimore, MD

Architekten RKW
Dusseldorf, Germany

WZMH
Toronto

Bregman Hammon
Toronto

HNTB
Alexandria, VA

■ Marty Coulter Studio

Marty Coulter Studio
10129 Conway Road
St. Louis / Missouri
63124

314.432.2721
314.432.2721 Cellular & Fax

Selected Projects

"Drachen Fire"
Roller Coaster at Busch
Gardens
Williamsburg, VA
Architect:
PGAV
St. Louis

Clients Include

Peckham, Guyton Albers &
Viets

Hellmuth, Obata &
Kassabaum

Sverdrup Interiors Division

Michael Fox, Inc.

Pearce Corporation

Busch Entertainment
Corporation

Ralston Purina Company

Anheuser-Busch
Companies, Inc.

The Forsythe Group, Inc.

Missouri Botanical Garden

Maritz Communications
Company

Robinson, Yesawich &
Pepperdine, Inc.
(Orlando)

Illustrating architectural
and sometimes not so
architectural subjects for
many St. Louis companies
since 1968

■ W. Kirk Doggett

Architectural Illustration
PO Box 1305
Suite 199
Brunswick / Maine
04011

207.729.4509

Renderings suited for use in design, presentation and marketing. Techniques include watercolor, graphite, and colored pencil. Computer generated pre-views are utilized to allow for client preferences and to assure satisfaction.

Former instructor of architectural rendering techniques at the Boston Architectural Center and Mount Ida College's Chamberlayne School of Design.

Member: American Society of Architectural Perspectivists

Architectural Clients Include

1. **Ward-Rovner Public Relations**
Boston

2. **Robert Durham / Architects**
Abilene, TX

Architectural Resources Cambridge
Cambridge, MA

Brim & Associates, Inc.
Danvers, MA

The Druker Company
Boston

The Flatley Company
Braintree, MA

The Hospitality Group
Northampton, MA

JSA Inc.
Portsmouth, NH

Wellesley Design Consultants
Wellesley, MA

Robert M. Wood Architects
Boston

Exhibitions

The Process of Architectural Perspective Rendering
Dana Gallery, Wellesley, MA
1991

ASAP Boston Members Show
World Trade Center, Boston
1990

■ Don Morgan

Don Morgan
8050 SW Valley View Court
Portland / Oregon
97225

503.292.4308

Techniques

Hardline and freehand ink
line drawings

Ink rendering with magic
marker and colored pencil
overlays

Black Prismacolor pencil
drawings

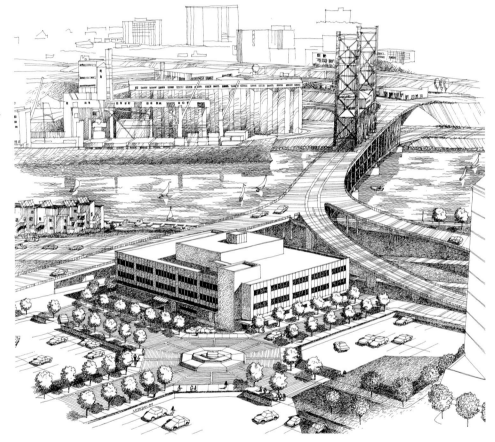

**Architectural Clients
Include**

**Broome Oringdulph
O'Toole Rudolf Boles &
Associates**
Portland, OR

**Wasserberger Benson
Partnership**
Portland, OR

Fletcher Farr Ayotte
Portland, OR

**Moreland Christopher
Myles Architects**
Portland, OR

Plaza / Foote Architects
Portland, OR

**Petersen-Kolberg &
Associates**
Wilsonville, OR

**Chilless Nielsen
Architects**
Portland, OR

**Otak Incorporated
Architects**
Lake Oswego, OR

Miller Cook Architects
Portland, OR

**Burns Clarke & Vogan
Architects**
Anchorage, AK

Other Clients Include

Summit Development

Prendergast & Associates

Hillman Properties
Northwest

■ Charles F. Giles

Charles F. Giles, Illustrator
Lilio Kalani Gardens
300 Wainani Way
Suite 1618
Honolulu / Hawaii
96815

808.922.1253

Experienced illustrator with architectural background specializing in architectural sketching and developmental drawings. Assists the client in visualizing a project throughout the design process, all the way to completion.

Samples and portfolio available upon request.

Architectural Clients Include

The Architects Collaborative
Cambridge, MA

Skidmore, Owings & Merrill
Boston

The Stubbins Associates
Cambridge, MA

RTKL Associates
Baltimore

Cambridge Seven Associates
Cambridge, MA

Sasaki Associates
Watertown, MA

Wimberly Allison Tong & Goo
Honolulu

Kajima Corporation
Tokyo, Japan

Stark Ventures Ltd.
Honolulu

Helber Hastert & Fee Planners
Honolulu

AM Partners Inc.
Honolulu

■ Shannon Graphics

Shannon Graphics
7862-D W Central Avenue
Toledo / Ohio
43617

419.841.7313
419.841.7917 Fax

Specializing in high quality, fast turn-around projects for both small and large businesses.

All projects computer modeled for precise view approval. Four views faxed to client for review and comments. Additional views available.

All traditional rendering techniques available. Special effects, night scenes, dimensional illustration, and detailed models professionally prepared to client's budget, schedule, and other specifications.

Complete photography services include negatives, transparencies, slides and prints.

Call for samples and full color brochure.

Selected Projects

NASA Space Station
Engineering
Huntsville, AL
Architect:
Gresham Smith & Partners
Birmingham, AL

Xerox Corporation
Rochester, NY
Architect:
SWBR Architects
Rochester, NY

National Institute of Health
Washington, DC
Architect:
The Kling Lindquist Partnership
Philadelphia, PA

William & Mary College
Syracuse, NY
Architect:
BBCG Architecture & Engineering
Auburn, NY

Brookfield Corporate Center
Sterling, VA
Developer:
Reynolds Metals
Vienna, VA

The Plain Dealer Newspaper
Cleveland, OH
Architect:
The Austin Company
Cleveland, OH

Fine Arts Center
Richmond, VA
Architect:
Wright, Cox & Smith
Richmond, VA

Services Include

Computer modeling

Sketch and detail renderings

Mass form to high detail models

Full service model shop.

Photography

■ Bill Evans

Bill Evans
804 2nd Avenue
Mezzanine
Seattle / Washington
98104

206.340.0655
206.682.7452 Fax

Techniques

Color
  Opaque watercolor
  Transparent watercolor
  Line with watercolor

Black on white
  Line
  Line with tones
  Full range of tones

**Architectural Clients
Include**

Arthur Erickson
Vancouver, Canada

NBBJ Group
Seattle

Fred Bassetti
Seattle

TRA
Seattle

Zimmer Gunsul Frasca
Portland, OR

Callison Partnership
Seattle

Demetri Balasari
New York City

Killingsworth Stricker
Long Beach, CA

**Bumgardner
Partnership**
Seattle

Jones & Jones
Seattle

LMN Architects
Seattle

Busch Gardens
Tampa, FL

San Diego Zoo
San Diego

Prec Institute Ltd
Tokyo, Japan

Work ranges from loose
conceptual sketches to
finished delineation in
color or black and white.
Full computerization
provides maximum
flexibility in view
selection and accuracy.

■ Thomas Wells Schaller, AIA

Schaller Architectural
Illustration
2112 Broadway, #407
New York / New York
10023

212.362.5524
212.362.5719 Fax

Awards

Hugh Ferriss Memorial
Prize 1988

Citation for Excellence
for *Architecture In
Watercolor*
AIA International Book
Awards 1991

Jurors' Award
*Architecture in Perspective
VI* 1991

Honor Awards
*Architecture in Perspective
I, II, III, IV, V, VI* 1986-91

Selected Project

Foley Square
United States Courthouse
Competition (1990)
New York City
40" x 30" watercolor
Architect:
**Kohn Pederson Fox
Associates**
New York City

■ Thomas Wells Schaller, AIA

Schaller Architectural
Illustration
2112 Broadway, #407
New York / New York
10023

212.362.5524
212.362.5719 Fax

Author of *Architecture in Watercolor* (Van Nostrand Reinhold 1990) and *Architecture of the Imagination* (Van Nostrand Reinhold 1992)

President Emeritus: The American Society of Architectural Perspectivists

Fellow: The Society of Architectural and Industrial Illustrators (Great Britain)

Architectural Clients Include

Kohn Pederson Fox Associates
New York City
London

Skidmore Owings & Merrill
New York City
Washington, DC
London

Keating Mann Jernigan Rottet
Los Angeles

Cesar Pelli & Associates
New Haven

Pei Cobb Freed & Partners
New York City

Perkins & Will
New York City

James Stewart Polshek & Partners
New York City

Hellmuth Obata Kassabaum
New York City

Nikken Sekkei International
New York City
Tokyo

Arquitectonica
Miami

Selected Project

Aquae Sulis 1991
Architect:
Thomas W. Schaller, AIA
18" x 18" watercolor

■ Ray Elliott Associates

Ray Elliott Associates
2560 Pine Cove Drive
Tucker / Georgia
30084

404.493.6307
404.493.6333 Fax

A hands-on, one-man approach to providing quality rendering at reasonable cost, with an emphasis on service. Producing images of high quality for more than 20 years.

Member: American Society of Architectural Perspectivists

Clients Include

Brown Design

Cunningham, Forehand, Mathews and Moore

The Facility Group

Fabrap

Georgia Power Company

BP Oil Company

Texaco Marketing USA

Turner Associates

Trammell Crow Company

Kajima International

Delta Air Lines

Smallwood, Reynolds, Stewart and Stewart

■ Ernest Burden III

Ernest Burden III
46 Eighth Avenue
Brooklyn / New York
11217

718.398.9166
718.857.9396 Fax

**Architectural Clients
Include**

Kohn Pedersen Fox
New York City

Ed Barnes/John Lee
New York City

I. M. Pei & Partners
New York City

H.O.K.
New York City

Conklin Rossant
New York City

Silver & Ziskind
New York City

Cooper + Robertson
New York City

**Cathedral of Saint John
the Divine**
New York City

Metro North Railroad
New York City

The Equitable
New York City

■ Michael P. Mastropolo

Mastropolo Arts, Inc.
60 Cannon Drive
Holbrook / New York
11741

516.589.8823

Established in 1974 as an
architectural rendering
firm specializing in high-
quality, full-color opaque
illustrations.

Member: American
Society of Architectural
Perspectivists

Specialties

Full color (edge to edge)

Color vignettes

Special effects (night
scenes)

Pen & ink

Pencil

Site plans

Elevations

Selected Project

BMW Manhattan
(offices and showroom)
New York City
Architect:
The Spector Group
North Hills, NY

Dudley Fleming

Dudley Fleming
Rockwood Sumner Grant
136 1/2 South Main
Studio One
Bowling Green / Ohio
43402

419.352.4740
419.353.4576 Fax

**Architectural Clients
Include**

The Collaborative Inc.
Toledo, OH
Tampa, FL

Wiley & Wilson Inc.
Richmond, VA

**Fanning / Howey
Associates, Inc.**
Celina, OH

MSKTD & Assoc., Inc.
Fort Wayne, IN

**Rooney and Clinger,
Architects**
Findlay, OH

Browning Day
Indianapolis, IN

Patrick Plus Associates
Columbus, OH

**Moake / Park
Associates**
Fort Wayne, IN

Bohm NBBJ
Columbus, OH

**Quinlivan Pierik &
Krause**
Syracuse, NY

URS Consultants
Columbus, OH

Selected Projects

1. INB Center
Fort Wayne, IN
Architect:
Schenkel Shultz Inc.
Fort Wayne, IN

2. Ramada
Renaissance Hotel
Richmond, VA
Architect:
**Glave Newman
Anderson**
Richmond, VA

1

2

Specializing in loose
design concept style
drawings, representing on
paper that which is in the
mind of the architect. Best
known for unique travel-
design-charrette service.
Member: ASAP

■ Gary Irish

Gary Irish Graphics
45 Newbury Street
Boston / Massachusetts
02116

617.247.4168
617.247.6476 Fax

Publications

Progressive Architecture

Architectural Record

New York Times
Sunday Magazine

Boston Magazine

Renderings Standards in
Architecture and Design

Architectural Clients Include

**Hugh Stubbins
Associates**
Cambridge, MA

**The Architects
Collaborative**
Cambridge, MA

**Massey Beatson
Rix-Trott & Carter**
Auckland, New Zealand

**Moshe Safdie &
Associates**
Cambridge, MA

**Frank E. Basil &
Company**
Athens, Greece

**W. Lyn Pinegar &
Associates**
Salt Lake City, UT

**McKugh Lloyd &
Associates**
Sante Fe, NM

**Shriver Holland &
Associates**
Norfolk, VA

Arrow Street
Cambridge, MA

Developed and taught
illustration courses at the
Harvard University
Graduate School of Design.
International clientele.

Finished renderings in pen
and ink on mylar with air-
brushed color. Able to meet
any deadline.

■ Steve Fritz

Steve Fritz Art Service
713 Fourth Street
Kalkaska / Michigan
49646

616.258.5528
616.258.9902 Fax

Exterior and interior renderings in various media, primarily watercolor and pencil. Services provided range from conceptual drawings through detailed finished presentation art.

Member: American Society of Architectural Perspectivists

Clients Include

The WBDC Group

Wieland-Davco Corp.

Wigen Tincknell
Meyer & Associates

Barckholtz Group Ltd.

Town & Country Cedar
Homes

Spruce Companies

Nicholas J. White, AIA

AAI, Inc.

GBKB Associates

Corbin Design

David Joyner
Fred Davis
PO Box 11173
Knoxville / Tennessee
37939-1173

615.584.8334
615.584.8334 Fax

Providing a full range of quality architectural illustration.

Member: American Society of Architectural Perspectivists; Tennessee Watercolor Society

Professional Affiliate: American Institute of Architects (East Tennessee Chapter)

Architectural Clients Include

Barber & McMurry, Inc.
Knoxville

Lockwood Greene, Inc.
Oak Ridge, TN

McCarty Holsaple McCarty
Knoxville

Upland Design Group, Inc.
Crossville, TN

Tennessee Valley Authority
Knoxville

Whittle Communications
Knoxville

Martin Marietta Energy Systems
Oak Ridge, TN

Brewer, Ingram, Fuller
Knoxville

Lewis Moore Group
Knoxville

Society of Environmental Graphic Designers Information

Alphabetical Listing

EGD

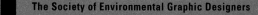

National Office:

47 3rd Street #201
Cambridge, MA 02141
617.577.8225

Attention:
Sarah Speare
Executive Director

Philosophy and Purpose

The Society of Environmental Graphic Designers (SEGD) is an international, non-profit, professional design organization devoted to promoting public awareness and professional development of the field of environmental graphic design. The society, founded in 1973, is a committed group of over 700 environmental graphic designers, industrial designers, architects, landscape architects, interior designers, researchers, educators, and manufacturers involved in three-dimensional visual communication design. Members' work ranges from exhibit design to large-scale sign systems to public art programs.

The environmental graphic designer plans, designs and specifies sign systems and other forms of visual communication in the built and natural environment. Environmental graphic design serves three basic functions: to assist users in negotiating through space, by identifying, directing, and informing; to visually enhance the environment; and to protect the safety of the public.

Membership

Membership is available in the following categories: Professional, Associate, Allied, Industry, Student, Institutional and Artisan. For more information, contact the Membership Coordinator.

Activities

The SEGD national conference is held each year in the summer at a Design School. Recent themes have included wayfinding, design collaboration, and design education. The conference includes lectures, workshops, an awards ceremony, and the annual Trade Show.

SEGD also holds Regional Meetings each year in different areas of the country. SEGD local mixers are organized by SEGD members across the United States year round.

Awards

The SEGD awards recognize outstanding achievements and significant contributions made to the profession in environmental graphic design. These awards are presented annually at the national conference.

SEGD Annual Design Competition: open to members and non-members, deadline for entries in May.

SEGD Fellow Award: presented for outstanding individual contribution to the Society and the field.

Insight Award: given to an individual or organization for promoting understanding and awareness of environmental graphic design.

Angel Award: given to an individual for promoting awareness of the values of the profession and for contributing to the programming and direction of SEGD.

Student Grant Award: presented to students pursuing a career in the field, deadline for applications is November.

Publications

Messages: The society's quarterly publication provides members and subscribers with lively feature articles exploring topics of the field. Also includes resource listings, in-depth profiles of members, technical column, advertising and SEGD membership news.

The Professional Firm Directory: This directory, published in 1991, profiles SEGD professional member firms.

The Resource Directory: This literature includes an SEGD membership directory, bylaws, and a complete bibliography.

Technical publications and bulletins: *The System of Classification* is part of SEGD's work to improve and standardize sign descriptions; *Sourcebook One "Materials and Technologies,"* is a comprehensive description of the materials, techniques and technology currently in use in the field; *Sourcebook Two "Specifications Guide,"* provides general guidelines to aid designers in specifying environmental graphics.

Special Programs

The SEGD Education Foundation, the charitable arm of the SEGD, was created to address critical and timely educational issues of interest to the profession. SEGD has been awarded four grants from the National Endowment for the Arts. With these grants, SEGDEF developed a Model Curriculum for environmental graphic design; created a new national system of recreation symbols signs for use in over 7,000 Federal, State and local parks; developed reproductive artwork and user guidelines for a national standard of Industrial and Consumer Safety Symbols to help safeguard the health and safety of millions of workers and consumers; and developed Part I: The Visual Collection of a national archive for environmental graphic design. For the results of the grants, contact the SEGD.

■ Tracy Turner Design Inc.

Tracy Turner Design Inc.
30 West 22nd Street
New York / New York
10010

212.989.0221
212.989.0249 Fax

Other Clients Include

Disney Development
Company

Suntec City Development
Pte Ltd.

Regent International
Hotels

Olympia & York

Carnegie Hall Corporation

Crocker & Company

Morgans Hotel Group
 Morgans
 The Royalton
 Paramount

Citicorp

Canadian Imperial Bank
of Commerce

Memorial Sloan-Kettering
Cancer Center

Philip Morris Companies

IBM Corporation

Rockrose Development

New Otani

**Architectural Clients
Include**

**Pei, Cobb, Freed &
Partners**
New York City

**Kohn Pedersen Fox
Associates**
New York City

**James Stewart
Polshek & Partners**
New York City

**Cooper Carry
Associates Inc.**
Washington DC

**Arata Isozaki &
Associates**
Tokyo
New York City

**Tsao & McKown
Architects**
New York City
Singapore

**Kohn Pedersen Fox
Conway Associates Inc.**
New York City

**Kallman McKinnell
& Wood**
Boston

A full service design firm
specializing in corporate
and project identity,
printed graphics,
architectural signage and
graphics, hotel amenities,
and product design, from
preliminary design to
fabrication and
installation management.

Photo Credits

Stephen C. Traves

Graham Uden

■ Wayne Hunt Design, Inc.

Wayne Hunt Design, Inc.
87 North Raymond Avenue
Suite 215
Pasadena / California
91103

818.793.7847
818.793.2549 Fax

Graphic design for
buildings, places, and
spaces, including:

Graphics Master Planning
Analysis & Programming
Nomenclature
Theme / Concept Design
Wayfinding
Signing Design
Construction Documents
Architectural Color
Retail Tenant Criteria

Selected Projects

Port of Long Beach
(gateway signing systems)
with Morris Deasy
Partners

City Walk
Universal City
(outdoor retail signing
& graphics program)
with Harmonica, Inc.

Pleasure Island
Walt Disney World
(themed graphics program)
with Walt Disney
Imagineering

California Plaza
(comprehensive signing
program for major mixed-
use complex)
with Don Clark Design

Old Pasadena
(pedestrian & automobile
signing system for themed
historic area)

Los Angeles County
Children's Court
(child-scale environmental
graphics & signing
program)

Knotts Camp Snoopy
at the Mall of America
(themed signing &
graphics program)

■ Wayne Hunt Design, Inc.

Wayne Hunt Design, Inc.
87 North Raymond Avenue
Suite 215
Pasadena / California
91103

818.793.7847
818.793.2549 Fax

Marketing and image
design for architects,
engineers, developers,
and the real estate
industry.

Brochures
Visual Identity Systems
Symbols & Logotypes
Presentations
Advertising
Newsletters
Project Identity
Exhibits

Clients Include

AIA / LA Associates

Archiplan

Architects Orange

Barasch Architects

Behr Browers Partnership

C.F. Braun

CHCG Architects

Devil's Gate Park

Ennis Brown House

Flewelling & Moody

Interior Design Inc.

Jacobs Engineering

Langdon & Wilson

Maguire Thomas Partners

NBS Lowry

O'Leary Terasawa Partners

Schaefer Dixon Associates

Takata Associates

Ziegler Kirven Parrish
Architects

■ Tainer Associates, Ltd.

Tainer Associates, Ltd.
213 West Institute Place
Suite 301
Chicago / Illinois
60610

312.951.1656
312.951.8773 Fax

Multi-disciplined design
studio specializing in
comprehensive
environmental and
graphic design programs
for architecture, real
estate, and furniture-
industry clients. Services
include corporate identity
and logo design; print
graphics; sales and
marketing programs;
and signage and exhibit
design.

Member: American
Institute of Architects,
American Society of
Architectural Perspectivists,
and American Center for
Design

Language Fluency: Italian,
French, & Spanish

Clients Include

GLS Development

Diversified Capital Group

Enrico Plati Development
Company

Daniele Development
Company

The Hoffman Group

Northfield Development
Company

Heitman Properties Ltd.

Pinuccio Ltd.

Rubloff, Inc.

Draper & Kramer Inc.

Park Barrington

United Development
Company

Gianni, Inc.

Estel, Inc.

Tanguay, Burke & Stratton

Embassy Suites Hotels

■ Clifford Selbert Design, Inc.

2067 Massachusetts
Avenue
Cambridge /
Massachusetts
02140

617.497.6605
617.661.5772 Fax

**Architectural Clients
Include**

**Hardy Holzman
Pfeiffer Associates**
New York City

**Herbert Newman
& Associates**
New Haven, CT

**Kallman McKinnell
& Wood**
Boston

**Robert A.M. Stern
Architects**
New York City

**Schwartz / Silver
Architects**
Boston

Services

Print Graphics

Environmental Graphics

Product Design

Package Design

Land Architecture

■ Clifford Selbert Design, Inc.

2067 Massachusetts
Avenue
Cambridge /
Massachusetts
02140

617.497.6605
617.661.5772 Fax

Publications

AIGA Annual
Abitare
Archive
Architecture
Architectural Record
Art New England
Communication Arts
Design World
Graphis
How
Identity
Interior Design
International Design
Landscape Architecture
Metropolitan Home
New York Times
Print
Progressive Architecture
SEGD Messages

■ Clifford Selbert Design, Inc.

2067 Massachusetts
Avenue
Cambridge /
Massachusetts
02140

617.497.6605
617.661.5772 Fax

Services

Print Graphics
Environmental Graphics
Product Design
Package Design
Land Architecture

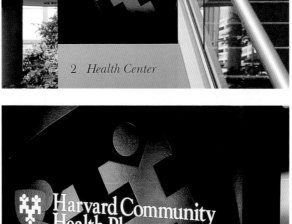

Awards

American Institute
of Graphic Arts

Art Directors Club
of New York

BSLA

CASE

Communication Arts

Creative Club of Boston

DESI

Graphis

Hatch

How

Massachusetts
Governors Design
Award

Photo / Design

Print

Typographers
International
Association

■ Carol Naughton + Associates, Inc.

Carol Naughton
213 West Institute Place
Chicago / Illinois
60610

312.951.5353
312.951.8369 Fax

Services

Graphic & Environmental Design

Planning Studies

Graphics Identity

Collateral Print Design

Exhibit Design

Thematic Design

Signage Design

Construction Documents

Selected Project

Exterior & Interior Signage
Corporate Headquarters
McDonald's Corporation
Oak Brook, IL

Comprehensive signage program for the hotel and nature trail on McDonald's 80-acre campus.

Exterior work included entrance identification as well as directional, regulatory, educational , and informational signs.

Interior work included directional, identification, and regulatory signs as well as signage for on-site restaurants, conference facilities, fitness center, and pool.

Approaching design as a collaborative process, with the belief that signage is most effective when it is an integral and integrated part of the built environment.

■ Robert Pease & Co., Inc.

Robert Pease & Co., Inc.
336 Castle Crest Road
Walnut Creek / California
94595-3402

510.820.0404
510.938.3788 Fax

A full-service graphic
design firm specializing in
all types of identity
systems for a wide variety
of clients.

Providing total marketing
design from trademarks to
all forms of brochure and
packaging graphics.

Member: Society of
Environmental Graphic
Designers; American
Institute of Graphic Arts;
and the Advisory Board
Western Art Directors
Club.

Clients Include

Asian Holdings

Fairchild Semiconductor

Eaton Semiconductor

Avis Rent-A-Car

Marietta Cellars

Palisades Vineyards

Grubb & Ellis Development

Perini Corporation

Pella Window Stores

The Carmel Workshop

Pacific Rim Development

Liberty Bank

■ Lighting Designers

International Association of Lighting Designers Information

IALD

The National Office:

18 East 16 Street
Suite 208
New York, NY 10003

212.206.1281
212.206.1327 Fax

The IALD has European and West Coast Committees which organize activities of regional interest to members.

Philosophy and Purpose

The International Association of Lighting Designers (IALD) was established in 1969 to represent the professional interests of independent lighting designers and to communicate the benefits of designed lighting. Members of the organization support the principle that professional lighting design involves aesthetics, behavioral considerations, and technical realities.

Under the requirements of membership and the Code of Ethics of the Association, IALD designers practice independently of commercial interests. Because they are compensated solely by professional fees, they are able to serve as impartial advocates of the interests of their clients.

Programs

Education is one of the major areas of focus for the IALD, from students entering the field to continuing education for those already in practice. The IALD's Intern Program allows design students to learn about architectural lighting design as a career through temporary or summer employment at design firms. Acceptance as an intern is dependent upon submission of a portfolio.

The Association is also becoming involved in the educational curricula available to students, with many members serving as instructors in university programs.

The annual IALD Awards Program honors lighting design that displays aesthetic achievement, technical expertise, and exemplifies a synthesis of architectural and lighting design. The Association publicizes award-winning projects as a way of educating the design community and the public about good lighting design. Slides of award-winning projects available for educational and editorial purposes.

The Energy Committee participates in the development of codes and standards relating to lighting. The IALD's Business Standards and Contracts Committee provides members with suggested business policies and procedures such as standard contracts, typical specification formats, and sound business practices.

Finally, the Association publishes a newsletter which in addition to news of individuals, lighting technology, and events of interest to the lighting community, contains articles relevant to the management of professional service firms.

Membership

Membership in the IALD has grown to 425 professionals. Voting membership is restricted to lighting designers from professional firms, with non-voting membership extended to design professionals from related fields.

Corporate members must have a minimum of four years of professional experience in architectural lighting design at the level of senior designer or above. Senior Associates must have at least two years of professional experience in architectural lighting design at the level of senior designer or above. Both are voting categories of membership, and in each case the applicant must be exclusively involved in lighting design. Those applying for Corporate and Senior Associate membership must submit portfolios for review by the Board of Directors.

Non-voting members include Associates, Educators, Students, and Press Affiliates. Associates are lighting designers with less experience than voting members, employees of lighting design firms, or practicing professionals in related fields whose activities include the occasional practice and/or appreciation of lighting design. Architects, interior designers, and engineers are typically Associate members.

Educator members devote the majority of their time to the teaching of lighting and/or related subjects, and student members must attend an accredited institution and concentrate their studies in lighting design or related fields. Press Affiliate memberships are available to those on the staffs of publications devoted to reporting information of interest to the field of architectural lighting design.

The Board of Directors may elect to bestow a Fellow designation on outstanding members of the profession and to elect Honorary Members. The by-laws of the Association are currently constituted so that membership at any level is not offered to those in manufacturing, sales, or distribution of equipment.

■ Carl Hillmann Associates

Carl Hillmann Associates
Lighting Design Inc.
118 East 25th Street
New York / New York
10010

212.529.7800
212.979.9108 Fax

Clients Include

**Cambridge Seven
Associates**
Cambridge, MA

**Gensler & Associates
Architects**
Los Angeles
Houston

**Gwathmey Siegel &
Associates**
New York City

HKS Architects
Dallas

3D/M
San Antonio, TX

WZMH
Toronto, Ontario, Canada

**American International
Group**
New York City

**Disney Development
Corporation**
Orlando, FL

The Taubman Company
Bloomfield Hills, MI

Offering imagination backed
by technical expertise and
accurate cost control in the
design of electric and
natural lighting. Equally
experienced in renovation
and new construction with
more than 500 corporate,
institutional, retail,
hospitality and residential
projects.

Photo Credits

1, 3. Zoom
     Photographics
2. ESTO
4. Paul Warchol

Selected Projects

1,3. First F.A. Building
DuPont Centre
Orlando, FL
Architect:
**Morris Aubry
Architects**
Houston

2. Offices of Anspach
Grossman Portugal
New York City
Architect:
**Samuel J. DeSanto &
Associates**
New York City

4. Landor Associates
New York City
Interior Designer:
Penney & Bernstein
New York City

USAA Headquarters
San Antonio, TX
Interior Designer:
The Whitney Group
Houston
Architect:
HKS Architects
Dallas

Offices of Ronald S. Lauder
New York City
Architect:
**Gwathmey Siegel &
Associates**
New York City

Disney Bonnet Lake
Golf Clubhouse
Orlando, FL
Architect:
**Gwathmey Siegel &
Associates**
New York City

■ Craig A. Roeder Associates, Inc.

Craig A. Roeder
Associates, Inc.
3829 North Hall Street
Dallas / Texas
75219

214.528.2300 Dallas
713.550.2300 Houston
214.521.2300 Fax

Illumination specialist
with fifteen years of
experience in lighting
design. Projects include
airports, hotels, corporate
offices, hospitals, retail
spaces, residences, clubs,
resorts, building facades,
malls, and roadways.

**Architectural Clients
Include**

**CRS Sirrine
Incorporated**
Houston

HKS Incorporated
Dallas

**Kohn Pederson Fox
Associates**
New York City

Lohan Associates
Chicago

Morris Architects
Houston

RTKL Associates
Dallas

■ Craig A. Roeder Associates, Inc.

Craig A. Roeder
Associates, Inc.
3829 North Hall Street
Dallas / Texas
75219

214.528.2300 Dallas
713.550.2300 Houston
214.521.2300 Fax

**Interior Design Clients
Include**

**Andre Staffelbach
Designs**
Dallas

**James Northcutt &
Associates**
Los Angeles

**Joszi Meskan
Associates**
San Francisco

Loyd • Paxton
Dallas

**Rita St. Clair
Associates**
Baltimore

**Walker-Hughes
Associates**
New York City

4

5

Other Clients Include

3M

Alexander Julian

American Airlines

Faison

Federal Home Loan Bank

GTE

Hilton Hotel

Humana Hospitals

Hyatt Hotel

IBM

Intercontinental Hotel

Lowes Hotel

Medical Cities Dallas

Methodist Hospital

Mirage

Omni Hotel

Ralph Lauren

Registry Hotels

State of Texas

Trammell Crow

United Nations

Services include general
consultation, budgeting,
lighting layout specification,
photometrics, control
systems, architectural detail
lighting, and custom
architectural and decorative
fixtures.

Photo Credits
4. Robt.
Ames Cook
5. Dan Forer

■ Design Decisions

Design Decisions
Jeffrey A. Milham, FIALD
35 Seacoast Terrace
Suite 19L
Brooklyn / New York
11235

718.769.7796
212.420.0377
718.769.7868 Fax

Selected Projects

1. Aetna Financial Division
Hartford, CT
Architect:
**Russell Gibson
Von Dohlen**
Farmington, CT

2. 919 Third Avenue
New York City
Architect:
**Skidmore, Owings &
Merrill**
New York City

3. New York State Senate
Albany, NY
Architect:
Mesick.Cohen.Waite
Albany, NY

The United Nations
New York City
Architect:
**Abramovitz-Harris-
Kingsland**
New York City

The University of Riyadh
Riyadh, Saudi Arabia
Architect:
**Hellmuth, Obata &
Kassabaum**
St. Louis

San Francisco
International Airport
Architect:
Gensler & Associates
San Francisco

Clients Include

Aetna Life & Casualty
  Capitol Avenue Offices
  Educational Institute
  Hartford Home Office
  Middletown Facility
  Windsor Facility

Berkshire Museum

Bicentennial Arts Center

Caltex Petroleum

Canadian Imperial Bank
of Commerce

Cigna Services Company

Citibank

Cointreau International

Covington & Burling

G.E. Capital

Georgetown University

Gilder Gagnon & Co.

Marshall University

Metromedia Inc.

NCR Corporation

Ogilvy & Mather

Olympia & York

Omni International Hotels

Pennsylvania State Capitol

Telerate Systems

Time Inc.

Touche Ross

Union Carbide Corporation

Vermont State Capitol

Since 1972: specializing
in architectural lighting
design for commercial,
institutional, and residential projects. Providing
complete services in sur-
vey, design concept and
layout, specification, bid
evaluation, drawing review
and field observation.

Photo Credits

1. Peter Vitale
2. Wolfgang Hoyt
3. Smithsonian
   Magazine

■ Gary Steffy Lighting Design

Gary R. Steffy, IES, IALD
315 East Eisenhower
Parkway
Suite 216
Ann Arbor / Michigan
48104

800.537.1230 Toll Free
313.747.6629 Fax

Energy, environmental, and ergonomic concerns considered paramount in achieving task, ambient, and architectural accent layers of lighting for comfort, productivity, and cost-effectiveness.

Selected Projects

Main Street
Ann Arbor, MI
Architect:
Johnson, Johnson & Roy, Inc.
Ann Arbor, MI

Brewery Park
(public spaces)
Detroit, MI
Architect:
Gensler & Associates
Denver, CO

Administrative Office
Land's End Company
Dodgeville, WI
Architect:
Martinson Architects
Green Bay, WI

Office Atrium, Conference Center, and Executive Offices
The Prudential Insurance Company
Roseland, NJ
Architect:
The Stubbins Associates
Boston

Offices / Steelcase Inc.
Kentwood, MI
Interior Designer:
Steelcase Design Group
Grand Rapids, MI

Photo Credits
Steelcase Photo Studio (top)
Robert Eovaldi (bottom)

■ Newcomb & Boyd

Newcomb & Boyd
One Northside 75
Atlanta / Georgia
30318-7761

404.352.3930
404.352.1826 Fax

Innovative specialists providing lighting design services tailored to the unique requirements of each project. Projects include hotels, corporate offices, public buildings, libraries, museums, banks, and showrooms.

Other system design services include audio-visual and acoustics; communications; security; energy management; fire protection; and mechanical / electrical.

1

2

Selected Projects

1. Hotel Nikko Atlanta
Architect:
**The Nichols
Partnership, Inc.**
Coral Gables, FL

2. Atlanta City Hall Complex
Architects:
**Muldawer-Moultrie •
Jova/Daniels/Busby •
Harris & Partners**
Atlanta

Country Club of Charleston
Charleston, SC
Architect:
LS3P Architects
Charleston, SC

KPMG Peat Marwick
Atlanta, GA
Interior Architect:
**Associated Space
Design, Inc.**
Atlanta

Law Library
Arizona State University
Tempe, AZ
Architects:
Scogin Elam & Bray
Atlanta
Leo A. Daly
Phoenix

Kilpatrick & Cody Attorneys
Atlanta, GA
Interior Designers:
Cooper Carry Studio
Atlanta

Photo Credit

1. Dan Forer
2. Kelly Holtz

■ Horton-Lees Lighting Design Inc.

200 Park Avenue South
Suite 1401
New York / New York
10003

212.674.5580

973 Market Street
Suite 650
San Francisco / California
94103

415.546.5630

Selected Projects

1. Rincon Center
San Francisco
Architect:
**Johnson Fain & Pereira
Associates**
Los Angeles

2. Dewey Ballantine
New York City
Architect:
Butler Rogers Baskett
New York City

3. McCarran International
Airport
Las Vegas
Architect:
TRA Consultants
Seattle

**Architectural Clients
Include**

Gensler & Associates
San Francisco
Los Angeles
Denver
Washington DC

**Hellmuth Obata &
Kassabaum**
New York City
Los Angeles
San Francisco

ISD Incorporated
New York City
Chicago
Los Angeles

**Kohn Pederson Fox
Associates, P.C.**
New York City

Lohan Associates
Chicago

**Pei Cobb Freed &
Partners**
New York City

**Skidmore, Owings &
Merrill**
New York City
Los Angeles
San Francisco

**The Architects
Collaborative**
Cambridge, MA
San Francisco

As specialists, we
concern ourselves with
lighting design and its
far-reaching effects on
all other disciplines

■ N. H. Fedder Associates, Inc.

N.H. Fedder Associates Inc.
10 Tulip Avenue
Floral Park / New York
11001

516.775.6529
718.343.3344
516.354.1171 Fax

Full-service architectural
lighting design firm
including custom fixture
design, optics, and
dimming. More than 275
commercial and
residential projects
completed to date.

1

2

3

Projects Include

Yokohama Convention
Center
Exterior lighting
Yokohama, Japan

Aquaduct Race Track
Jamaica, NY

Sky Chef's Restaurants:
　Newark Airport
　Palm Beach Airport

First Boston
5 World Trade Center
New York City

Air Vita
Phoenix Airport
Phoenix, AZ

NBC Third Floor News Room
New York City

Chambrel at Westlake
Westlake, OH

American Airlines
Admirals' Club:
　Kennedy Airport
　LaGuardia Airport
　(New York City)
　Logan Airport,
　(Boston, MA)

American Museum of
Natural History
(Phases I, II, & III)
New York City

Hyatt Key West
Key West, FL

Photo Credit
1. Scott Frances
2,3. George D. Miller

Selected Projects

1. Don Carter's Office
New York City
Interior Designer:
IFA
New York City

2, 3. Sky Chef's Restaurant
Ft Lauderdale Airport
Interior Designer:
The Office of Phil George
New York City

■ Specialized Services

**Boston Chapter of Industrial Designers Society of America
Information**

SP

IDSA Boston Chapter:

112 Beech Street
Roslindale, MA 02131

617.469.5416

Attention:
Elizabeth Goodrich
Chairman

IDSA is the national organization of professionals who design products, equipment, instruments, furniture, toys, transportation, packaging, exhibits, environments, and information systems. Founded in the 1930's, IDSA promotes the design profession, lobbies for design related issues, and provides services and programs to help industrial designers continue their professional development.

The Boston Chapter of IDSA holds periodic meetings focusing on design issues, presentations by design luminaries, new technologies, and related arts and cultural developments. We seek to provide an opportunity for design professionals to meet and exchange information in the interest of building the design community in Boston. We also distribute a newsletter which discusses our upcoming events for the season and sponsor seminars for professional development.

Membership in IDSA is broken into five categories: Member, Associate Member, and International Member, which require that the candidate have an undergraduate degree in design or ten years of experience in the field, Student Member; and Affiliate Member, which does not require a design background.

IDSA sponsors a National Conference and District Conferences each year. Held in the summer, the *IDSA National Conference* emphasizes design interaction with presentations by pacesetters on design, creativity, business, and cultural issues. The 1992 National Conference will be held in San Francisco. All IDSA members are eligible to enter the *Industrial Design Excellence Awards* which are held each spring. IDSA announces the winners at the National Design Conference and publicizes the winning entries to the design community along with business, trade, and general press.

IDSA National publishes the Directory of Industrial Designers; periodicals including the journal Innovation, the newsletter Design Perspectives, and annual studies on design management.

IDSA provides an *Ethics Advisory Council* which advises in matters regarding ethical conduct and moderates in ethical disputes. The *Code of Ethics* is published in the IDSA directory each year.

■ Valley Bronze of Oregon

Valley Bronze of Oregon
PO Box 669
307 West Alder Street
Joseph / Oregon
97846

503.432.7551
800.472.3970 Toll Free
503.432.0255 Fax

Artist Clients Include

Mick Brownlee

George Carlson

Chester Fields

Jan Fisher

Dorothy Fowler

Lorenzo Ghiglieri

Veryl Goodnight

Walt Matia

Jacques & Mary
Regat

Richard Stiers

Stan Wanlass

A full-service art foundry specializing in the production of monumental sculpture for architectural settings. Capable of undertaking point-up enlargements and model making. Casting in bronze, sterling silver, fine silver, stainless steel, and cast iron. On-site stone and wood base making, engineering, and installation services available.

Photo Credit

David Jensen

■ Dennis Earl Moore Productions, Inc.

137 Atlantic Avenue
Brooklyn Heights / New York
11201

718.875.8024
718.522.4358 Fax

Makes the use of film and electronic imaging available as raw building materials important to the architect and environmental designer. Focus of independent and collaborative work is twofold:

Video: The use of multi-image video as a 3-dimensional component that complements and articulates public spaces.

Film: Concept, design, and production of hybrid large scale film presentations that interpret, inspire, and entertain within defined spaces such as orientation areas, IMAX/OMNIMAX theaters, museums, and World's Fairs.

Worldwide project experience. Strength in concept development encourages participation from project inception.

Selected Projects

1. *Flyers*
First IMAX/OMNIMAX narrative film

2. *Video Lab*
60 Screen Video Assemblage research setting simulation

3, 5. *Videohenge* Panorama 120 Screen, 3-Dimensional Walkthru Video Environment

4. *Living Planet*
IMAX/OMNIMAX film (70mm - 75'x100' screens)

Reflections
1984 Louisiana World's Fair Unique Dual 35mm Over/Under Screen Format

RoboShoe
Six Axis Robotic Arm With Video Camera in Combination With 36 Monitor Stand-On-Floor Environment

Meet the Biospherians
Interactive Video Theater Incorporating Live Performance

Clients Include

SC Johnson Wax

1984 World's Fair
Petroleum Industries Pavilion

Nike, Inc.

Conoco, Inc./DuPont

Smithsonian Institution
National Air & Space Museum

Space Biospheres Ventures
Biosphere 2

■ Shenandoah Timberworks, Inc.

Shenandoah
Timberworks, Inc.
1005 South 5th Street
Hamilton / Montana
59875

406.363.6491

Custom timber framing,
classic joinery, and
innovative applications,
including the bonding of
timbers to metal frames
for a more pleasing and
satisfying appearance.
Handcrafted workmanship
for both residential and
commercial design.

**Architectural Clients
Include**

**Hagman & Yaw
Architects**
Aspen, CO

Dynamic Design
Hamilton, MT

Stoskopf / Architects
Tulsa, OK

Photo Credit
William Meriwether

Other Clients Include

Hansen Construction, Inc.

Timberhouse Post & Beam

The Hilley Company

■ Karman Ltd.

Karman Ltd.
Architectural Products
7931 Deering Avenue
Canoga Park/California
91304

818.888.3818
818.888.3029 Fax

Manufactures and installs high quality products fabricated from aluminum, brass, copper, stainless steel, glass, acrylic, and fiberglass.

Illuminated and non-illuminated products for interior and exterior placement: directories, pylons, letters, and neon, produced through processes that include art preparation, phototypesetting, silk screening, spray painting, gold leafing, etching, and sandblasting.

Specializes in complete signage projects for hotels, hospitals, schools, shopping malls, airports, parking structures, and libraries.

Selected Projects

1, 2. Dolphin Hotel
Orlando, FL
Architect:
Michael Graves
New York City
Graphic Designer:
Arias Associates
Palo Alto, CA

3. Manulife Insurance Building
Los Angeles
Architect:
A.C. Martin & Associates
Los Angeles

4. Fossil Creek
Fort Worth, TX
Developer:
Woodbine Development Company
Dallas

UCSF Medical Center & Library
Graphic Designer:
Cummings Design
Santa Monica, CA

Chicago Hilton & Towers
Interior Designer:
Frank Mingus Design
Atlanta

South Coast Plaza
Newport Beach, CA
Architect:
Architect Pacifica Ltd.
Newport Beach, CA

Awards

IBD Gold 1980

IBD Silver 1983

PRINT Casebook Certificate of Excellence 1984

SEGD Bronze 1991

■ Ken Lieberman Laboratories, Inc.

Ken Lieberman
Laboratories, Inc.
118 West 22nd Street
New York / New York
10011

212.633.0500
212.675.8269 Fax

Other Clients Include

AT&T

American Express

Eastman Kodak Company

Grumman Corporation

National Audubon Society

Sports Illustrated
Magazine

Madison Square Garden

Kellogs Corporation

Kimberly Clark Corporation

Bristol Myers Squibb

Nikon Inc.

Olympus Corporation

Life Magazine

Merck & Company

**Architectural Clients
Include**

**Hellmuth, Obata &
Kassabaum**
St. Louis, MO

**Skidmore, Owings &
Merrill**
New York City

The Spector Group
North Hills, NY

Eisenman Architects
New York City

Olympia & York
New York City

Custom laboratory creating
photographic prints to any
size from art, renderings,
slides and negatives.
Offered as well are
complete framing and
mounting services, and an
extensive selection of
images suitable for wall
decor and display.

■ William Hemmerdinger

William Hemmerdinger
42-240 Green Way
Suite D
Palm Desert / California
92260

619.340.5460

Bronze, stone, mosaic, wood, or fabric site-specific, mixed-media paintings, sculpture, and fountains. Established practice collaborating with architects, interior designers, landscape architects, and developers, as well as foundries and technicians in all phases, from initial concept, blueprints, and scale models, through final installation details.

Collaborations have produced unique combinations of contemporary art with antiquities and have included reconfiguring environments that have existing artworks. Applications appropriate for residential, commercial, or public settings.

1

Collections

1. Private Residence
The Vintage Club
Indian Wells, CA
Architect:
Howard Oxley, AIA
San Diego
Landscape Architect:
Ronald Gregory & Assoc.
Palm Desert, CA
Interior Design:
Jeff Benedict, ASID
Newport Beach, CA

2. Stouffer's Esmeralda Resort
Indian Wells, CA
Architect:
Hornsberger Associates
San Francisco
Interior Design:
Al Veres
Sea Ranch, CA

3. Private Residence
Cooper Garden Fountain
Riverside, CA

2

3

■ Model Makers

American Engineering Model Society Information

Alphabetical Listing

MM

National Office:

American Engineering Model Society
The Engineering Center
One Walnut Street
Boston, MA 02108

617.248.1928

Attention:
Ms. Paula Golden
Executive Director

Philosophy and Purpose

The American Engineering Model Society (AEMS) promotes and serves the interests of professional model-makers worldwide.

The objectives of the society are:

- To provide for the interchange of ideas among its members; to arrange for the collection and dissemination of information related to the use of physical models through publications, papers, seminars, and expositions.

- To educate the industrial public regarding the uses, applications, and advantages of physical models in industry, science, and government.

- To recognize those individuals engaged in the use of physical models and especially their outstanding accomplishments.

- To actively engage in a cooperative effort with other societies with mutual interests.

- To engage in a cooperative effort with the educational community to develop modeling as a vocation.

Membership

Membership in AEMS is open to individuals or organizations with an interest in the professional fabrication or use of physical models.

There are four grades of personal membership: Student, Individual, Emeritus and Honorary. There are two grades of organizational membership: Sustaining and Sponsoring.

To provide greater participatory opportunity among regional members the AEMS is endeavoring to establish a network of regional chapters. Currently chapters exist in: Milwaukee/Wisconsin, Chicago

Organizing efforts are underway in: Boston, San Francisco, Atlanta, Dallas, Seattle

Awards

Outstanding Contribution Award
Awarded at the discretion of the Board of Directors in recognition of exemplary career service to the AEMS and outstanding contribution to its success.

President's Award
Awarded at the discretion of the Board of Directors in recognition of exemplary contributions in the use and promotion of scale models and to the success of the AEMS.

Highest Achievement Award
Awarded at the discretion of the Executive Committee for superlative contributions in the use and promotion of scale models.

Rasmussen Memorial Scholarship Award
"The Ronald A. Rasmussen Memorial Scholarship Award is to be given annually to a second year model-making student best exemplifying the unselfish character and integrity of Ronald Rasmussen. Sponsored by the AEMS and funded by private donations from across the nation, the goal of this gift is to continue Ron Rasmussen's motivation, encouragement, and support of the model-makers of tomorrow."

Activities

National Convention:
Indian Lakes Resort
Chicago, Illinois, May 15-16, 1992

Publications

AEMS Newsletter (6 issues/year)

Membership Directory (annual)

Catalogue of Services (annual)

Model-making Bibliography (annual)

Seminar Papers (by event)

Special Programs

- Reference Library

- "Adventures in Scale Modeling"— PBS-TV series

- Education Symposia at design schools & technical colleges nationwide

- Professional Development Workshops

- Rasmussen Memorial Scholarship Fund

- NICET Certification

- Member Model Photo Display at National Seminar

Miscellaneous

Special Interest Groups:

To address the growing diversity and complexity of professional model making skills, the AEMS has created Special Interest Groups (SIG's). Each SIG acts as a committee reporting to the National Board of Directors issues of interest and concern to that SIG. Currently SIG's represent the following areas:

Architecture
Forensic/Litigation
CADD/CAM
Piping
Display/Exhibit
Prototype
Engineering
Special Effects

■ Einer Model Company

Einer Model Company
412 113th Street
Arlington / Texas
76011

817.633.5644
817.633.3759 Fax

**Architectural Clients
Include**

JPJ Architects
Dallas

**Trammell Crow
Company**
Dallas
Austin
Charlotte, NC
Chicago

Dahl Braden PTM Inc.
Dallas

**Harper Kemps Clutts &
Parker**
Dallas

Ray Bailey Architects
Houston

**Harold E. Kaemmerling
Architect**
Lufkin, TX

RTKL
Dallas

Other Clients Include

Wyndham Hotel Company

Sea World of Texas

LARC
(Dallas)

Island Development
(Corpus Christi, TX)

Freeman Exhibit Company

Selected Project

Information Center
Seaworld of Texas
San Antonio, TX
Client:
Sea World of Texas
San Antonio, TX

■ SCALE

SCALE
Harold Kalmus
Barry Lehr
111-117 Federal Street
Philadelphia /
Pennsylvania
19147

215.462.9222
215.462.9310 Fax

Selected Project

2121 Pennsylvania Avenue
Washington DC
Architect:
Michael Graves
Princeton, NJ

**Architectural Clients
Include**

Bell Atlantic Properties
Philadelphia

Circle Development
Washington DC

**Geddes Brecher Qualls
Cunningham**
Philadelphia

**Gerald D. Hines
Interests**
New York City

The Hillier Group
Princeton, NJ

**The Kling-Lindquist
Partnership**
Philadelphia

The Linpro Company
Philadelphia

**Michael Graves
Architect**
Princeton, NJ

**Peter Marino &
Associates**
New York City

**Thompson Ventulett
Stainback & Associates**
Atlanta

Architectural models
of exceptional quality
and detail.

Photo Credit
© Joe Aker 1990

■ Joseph Hutchins & Associates

Joseph Hutchins &
Associates
55 West 13th Street
5th Floor
New York / New York
10011

212.366.0828
212.366.0829 Fax

Selected Project

1. IBM Building
Baltimore
Scale 1" = 8'
Architect:
SOM
Washington, DC

2. Detail of Roof
with brass truss and
cast metal railings

3. Detail of cantilever
with laser-cut facades

Clients Include

**Skidmore, Owings &
Merrill**
New York City
Washington, DC

The Switzer Group, Inc.
New York City

**Helmuth Obata &
Kassabaum**
New York City

Perkins & Will
New York City

**Davis Brody &
Associates**
New York

Fox & Fowle
New York

**Hambrecht Terrell
International**
New York

BMW
New Jersey

Bechtel Corporation
New York City

Chase Manhattan Bank
New York City

Mobil Oil
New York City

Services Include

Interior and exterior
models

Site models

Prototypes

■ Paragon Models Inc.

Paragon Models Inc.
10812 Beech Creek Drive
Columbia / Maryland
21044-1023

410.740.4069
800.6.CADCAM Toll Free
410.290.8191 Fax

Specialties include in-house CAD/CAM fabrication, resin casting, and fiber optic lighting systems. Diversified international experience.

Architectural Clients Include

RTKL Associates
Baltimore, MD

Joseph Alfandre Company
Rockville, MD

Marriott Retirement Services
Ballston, VA

LDR / International
London
Columbia, MD

Charles E. Smith Company
Arlington, VA

Columbia Design Collective
Columbia, MD

Rivermead Homes
Fairfax, VA

Crestwood Homes
Greenbelt, MD

Whiting - Turner
Towson, MD

Photo Credits

James M. Burns
(top)
PMI (bottom)

Kenneth M. Champlin

Kenneth Champlin &
Associates
85 Willow Street
New Haven / Connecticut
06511

203.562.8400
203.562.9625 Fax

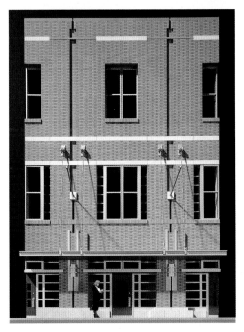

**Architectural Clients
Include**

Centerbrook Architects
Essex, CT

**Jacobs Visconi &
Jacobs**
Cleveland, OH

The Kaempfer Company
Washington, DC

**Kohn Pederson Fox
Associates**
New York City

**Konover / Kenny
Associates**
Hartford, CT

**Miglin-Beitler
Developments**
Chicago

**Olympia & York
Developments**
New York City

Cesar Pelli & Associates
New Haven, CT

**Prentice & Chan,
Olhausen**
New York City

**Skidmore, Owings &
Merrill**
New York City

HKS
Dallas

**The Kling-Lindquist
Partnership, Inc.**
Philadelphia

Associate member AIA
and CSAIA

■ Knoll Architectural Models, Inc.

Knoll Architectural Models
15752 Crabbs Branch Way
Rockville / Maryland
20855-2620

301.258.5212
301.670.9754 Fax

Professional model maker since 1965. Precisely scaled architectural models brought to life.

Affiliated with the American Institute of Architects, the SMPS, and the American Society of Landscape Architects.

Clients Include

Wisnewski, Blair & Associates, Ltd.

EDAW, Inc.

Skidmore, Owings & Merrill

Notter, Finegold & Alexander

Hartman-Cox Architects

Daniel, Mann, Johnson & Mendenhall

Keyes, Condon & Florence

Davis & Carter, PC

Leo A. Daly Company

Henningson, Durham & Richardson, Inc.

CHK Architects & Planners

Marriott Corporation

STV-HD Nottingham

Hugh Newell Jacobsen, FAIA

O'Brien & Gere Engineers, Inc.

Specialties Include

Architectural

Land Planning

Site Development

■ Scale Models Unlimited

111 Independence Drive
Menlo Park / California
94025

800.DIAL.SMU Toll Free
415.324.2111 Fax

320 West Ohio Street
Chicago / Illinois
60610

312.943.8160
312.943.9366 Fax

Selected Projects

1. 77 West Wacker Drive
Chicago
Developer:
The Prime Group
Chicago

2. 343 Sansome
San Francisco
Developer:
Hines Interests
San Francisco

3. 125 High Street
Boston
Developer:
Spaulding & Slye
Boston

4. **LaserCAMM** ™
Computer-driven laser
cutter manufactured by
Scale Models Unlimited
to reduce cost, shorten
construction time, and
create the highest level
of detail and accuracy
obtainable.

**Architectural Clients
Include**

John Burgee Architects
New York City

EDAW
Atlanta

Gensler & Associates
San Francisco

**Hellmuth, Obata &
Kassabaum, Inc.**
San Francisco

**Johnson Fain & Pereira
Associates**
Los Angeles

**Jung / Brannen
Associates, Inc.**
Boston

Caesar Pelli
New Haven, CT

Perkins & Will
Chicago

**Skidmore, Owings &
Merrill**
San Francisco
Chicago

Robert A.M. Stern
New York City

Services

Foam Topographic Models

Architectural Study Models

Site Plan Models

Detailed Marketing Models

Photo Superimposition

Laser Cutting

LaserCAMM ™ Sales

Photo Credits

Steve Rosenthal
Hedrich-Blessing

■ Richard Tenguerian

Tenguerian Models, Inc.
419 Lafayette Street
New York / New York
10003

212.228.9092
212.228.9093
212.228.6252 Fax

Architectural Clients Include

Ellerbe Becket, Inc.
New York City

John Burgee Architects
New York City

Perkins & Will
New York City

Skidmore, Owings & Merrill
New York City

Pei Cobb Freed & Partners
New York City

Battery Park City Authority
New York City

Edward Callan Interests
Houston

Gerald D. Hines
New York City

Olympia & York Properties
New York City

The Trump Organization
New York City

Recommendations

"Skill and dedication... equal to the highest standard. He...has always responded with a product of the finest quality."
William Pederson
Kohn, Pederson, Fox Associates PC

"Richard...is extremely dedicated and talented... I would recommend him as a model maker without hesitation."
Richard Meier
Richard Meier & Partners Architects

"Richard's skill and artistry are unmatched and his dedication to his craft rare."
Robert Venturi
Venturi, Rauch, Scott Brown, Inc.

"We...wholeheartedly recommend Tenguerian Models for any model job."
Bernard Tschumi
Bernard Tschumi Architects

Photo Credit

Jock Pottle

■ Dimensional Productions

Stephen H. Ford
669 Melvin Drive
Baltimore / Maryland
21230

410.837.7138
410.547.1144

Quality model building for more than 27 years. Provider of a full range of architectural model building services, from very high quality styrofoam contour maps and study models to presentation- and museum-quality finished models.

Developer of a unique process for producing styrofoam contour maps efficiently, with greater accuracy and surface smoothness than otherwise available.

Clients Include

1. Smithsonian Institution
2. RTKL Inc.
EDAW Inc.
United States Army
United States Navy
United States Coast Guard
S.O.M.
HOK
Westinghouse, Inc.
Gould, Inc.
Ayers, Saint, Gross Inc.

1

2

Photo Credit

Dave Whitcomb

■ Real Model, Inc.

Edward Leftwich, AIA
280 Elizabeth Street
Suite C104
Atlanta / Georgia
30307

404.524.4458
404.522.0267
404.522.4417 Fax

Clients Include

Targeted Communications
Corporation

Forest City Ratner

Pfizer

The RTC Group

Cousins Properties Inc.

The Landmarks Group

Rosser Fabrap
International

Thompson Ventulett
Stainback & Associates

GLG

Newington Cropsey
Foundation

Atlanta Olympic
Committee

1

2   3

Selected Projects

1. Atlanta Motor Speedway
Scale: 3/32" = 1'
1500 Tara Place
Condominiums
Architect:
Niles Bolton Associates
Atlanta

2, 3. GLG Grand
Atlanta
Scale: 1/16" = 1'
Architect:
**Rabun Hatch &
Associates**
Atlanta

Metrotech Center
Brooklyn, NY
Clients:
Forest City Ratner
New York City
The RTC Group
Arlington, VA

Greensboro Coliseum
Greensboro, NC
Client:
**Rosser Fabrap
International**
Atlanta

Convention Center
Ocean City, MD
Client:
**Rosser Fabrap
International**
Atlanta

Delta City
Robo Cop III
Client:
OCP Pictures
Atlanta

Photo Credit
Jennifer Almand

■ Peter McCann

Peter McCann
Architectural Models Inc.
49 Niagara Street
3rd Floor
Toronto / Ontario
Canada M5V 1C2

416.366.0326
416.366.0326 Fax

Selected Projects

1. Moscow Business
Center
Moscow
Architect:
**Zeidler Roberts
Partnership**
Toronto

2. Magna World
Headquarters
Toronto
Architect:
**Moffat Kinoshita
Associates Inc.**
Toronto

**Architectural Clients
Include**

Arthur Erickson
Los Angeles

Bramalea Ltd.
Toronto

Bregman & Hamann
Toronto

Cadilac Fairview
Toronto

Dewberry & Davis
Fairfax, VA

Howden Canada
Toronto

IBM
Toronto

Marathon Realty
Toronto

Olympia & York
Toronto

Perez Corporation
Ottawa, Canada

The Rouse Company
Baltimore, MD

Specializing in
architectural models and
prototypes. Using laser
cutting and metal etching
techniques to provide the
highest precision for
presentation worldwide.

Photo Credits

Lenscape Inc. (top)

Panda Associates
(bottom)

■ Exhibitgroup

Stan Zalenski
8401 Ambassador Row
Dallas / Texas
75247-4697

214.630.1441
214.630.6490 Fax

Exquisitely precise architectural models crafted for many of the world's leading developers and architects, incorporating meticulous design and an unsurpassed sense of reality.

Creative hands and minds prevail, whether the project requires the miniaturization of ten thousand acres to topographic precision or expressing a subtle architectural element.

State-of-the-art techniques blended with traditional artistry and craftsmanship.

Architectural Clients Include

Skidmore, Owings & Merrill
New York City

Kohn Pederson Fox
New York City

Kevin Roche, John Dinkeloo Associates
Hamden, CT

Cesar Pelli & Associates
New Haven, CT

DeStefano / Goettsch
Chicago, IL

Keyes Condon Florance Architects
Washington, DC

The Irvine Company
Irvine, CA

Selected Project

191 Peachtree Tower
Atlanta
Architect:
John Burgee Architects
New York City

Photo Credit

© Aker Photography

■ Jeff Blanton

Jeff Blanton Photography
5515 South Orange Avenue
Orlando / Florida
32809

407.851.7279
407.857.4272 Fax

Publications

Audio/Video Interiors
Private Clubs Magazine
Better Homes & Gardens
Times Mirror, Inc.
Meredith Corporation
Planning Ideas

■ Richard Mandelkorn

Richard Mandelkorn
Photography
309 Waltham Street
West Newton /
Massachusetts
02165

617.332.3246
617.332.3238 Fax

Selected Projects

1. Private Residence
Waterford, VA
Architect:
**Perry Dean Rogers &
Partners**
Boston

2. Private Residence
LaJolla, CA
Interior Designer:
The Cooper Group
Boston

Publications

Architectural Digest
Architectural Lighting
Architectural Record
Architecture
Historic Preservation
Interior Design
Interiors
Landscape Architecture
Nikkei Architecture
Photographis
Progressive Architecture

■ William E. Miller

William E. Miller
239 Park Avenue South
Suite 5C
New York / New York
10003

212.477.5452

Award-winning photography of residences, corporate contract interiors, exteriors, shopping centers, the urban and suburban landscapes. Using strong composition, graphics, and color to create a special sense of space and light.

Clients Include

Castro Blanco Piscionari Associates

Cross & Brown

Cushman & Wakefield

Dalsimer Baron Group

Devon Properties

Edward S. Gordon

Helmsley-Spear

Integrated Resources

Jones Lang Wootten

Mendik Realty Co.

Schroder Real Estate

SCR Design

SPGA

Turner Construction

Williams Real Estate

Winthrop Organization

■ Eric Oxendorf

Eric Oxendorf
1442 N. Franklin Place
PO Box 92337
Milwaukee / Wisconsin
53202

414.273.0654
414.273.1759

An artist and technician specializing in exterior and interior architectural images, panoramic, 360°, and aerial photography. Provides distinctive images that capture the character of the project and materials. More than 18,000 stock images available. FAA licensed pilots. *Domes of America* poster sent upon request.

Degree in fine art. Work exhibited in numerous one-man and group exhibitions, as well as private and corporate collections.

Visits more than 250 cities each year, giving clients the ability to share travel expenses when projects are in the same locale.

Member: American Society of Magazine Photographers.

■ Eric Oxendorf

Eric Oxendorf
1442 North Franklin Place
PO Box 92337
Milwaukee / Wisconsin
53202

414.273.0654
414.273.1759 Fax

Publications

Architectural Digest
AIA Journal
Wisconsin Architect
Florida Architect
Inland Architect
Progressive Architecture
Historic Preservation
Architectural Record
Time
INC. Magazine
New York Times
Business Week
Chicago Magazine
Home
Interiors
Photo Methods
Industrial Photography
USAir Magazine

■ Craig Collins

Craig Collins
2359 ¹/₂ Loma Vista Place
Los Angeles / California
90039

213.662.3271
213.662.3261 Fax

Clients Include

Security Pacific Bank
Glendale Federal Bank
Kaiser Permanente
Pacific Rim Properties
Rigney Development
RTK & Associates
R&B Realty Group

Providing photography
to the architectural,
corporate, and graphic
design communities,
merging an intimate
understanding of color
and design with
interpretive vision to
achieve the unique
communication needs of
each project.

Selected Project

Horton Plaza
San Diego
Engineers:
**Robert Engelkirk
Consulting Structural
Engineers Inc.**
Los Angeles

■ Tom Bernard

Tom Bernard Photography
586 Conestoga Road
Berwyn / Pennsylvania
19312

215.296.9289

Publications

Architecture &
Urbanism

Architectural
Record

Architecture

Baumeister

Builder

Designer Specifier

Interior Design

Interiors

L'Architecture
d'Aujourd'hui

Progressive
Architecture

Specializing in
architectural and interior
photography. Emphasizes
close collaboration with
architects and designers.

For additional work, see
A/DC 1 and 2.

■ Warren Jagger

Warren Jagger
150 Chestnut Street
Providence / Rhode Island
02903

401.351.7366
401.421.7567 Fax

Selected Projects

1. Joseph Abboud
Boston
Designer:
**Bentley LaRosa
Salasky**
New York City
(As featured in
Architectural Record,
September 1991)

2. The Hudson Companies
Providence, RI
Architect:
Ekman, Arp & Snider
Warwick, RI

3. The Pavilions at
Buckland Hills
Hartford, CT
Architect:
**Cambridge Seven
Associates**
Cambridge, MA

1

■ Warren Jagger

Warren Jagger
150 Chestnut Street
Providence / Rhode Island
02903

401.351.7366
401.421.7567 Fax

**Architectural Clients
Include**

**The Architects
Collaborative**
Cambridge, MA

ADD Inc.
Cambridge, MA

Boston Properties
Boston
Washington, DC

CUH2A
Princeton, NJ

**Graham Gund
Architects**
Cambridge, MA

**Homart Development
Company**
Chicago

Herman Miller Inc.
Zeeland, MI

**Jung Brannen
Associates, Inc.**
Boston

**Skidmore, Owings &
Merrill**
New York City

**The Stubbins
Associates**
Cambridge, MA

Publications

Architecture

Architectural Digest

Architectural Record

Contract

Metropolitan Home

Interiors

Interior Design

Progressive
Architecture

Restaurant &
Hotel Design

VM & SD

2

3

■ Jay Hyma

Hyma Photography
40907 Via Ranchitos
Fallbrook / California
92028

619.723.4700
619.723.4800 Fax

Creating interior and exterior architectural photographs for print and publication.

Portfolio available upon request. See A/DC 2 for additional work.

■ Anton Grassl

Anton Grassl
5 Sycamore Street
Cambridge /
Massachusetts
02140

617.876.1321

Architectural Clients Include

Arrowstreet, Inc.
Somerville, MA

Jeremiah Eck, AIA
Boston

Goody / Clancy & Associates
Boston

Payette Associates
Boston

Sasaki Associates
Watertown, MA

HKT Architects
Cambridge, MA

Machado & Silvetti Associates
Boston

Masters & Sargent
Boston

Other Clients Include

Cutler Associates

Harvard University
Graduate School of Design

Clifford Selbert Design

Boston Properties

Spaulding & Slye

Logowitz & Moore Design
Associates

Publications

Architecture

Landscape Architecture

Professional Builders
Magazine

The Boston Globe

Design Times

Harvard Magazine

■ Don Wheeler

Don Wheeler,
Photographer
Studio C
1933 South Boston Avenue
Tulsa / Oklahoma
74119

918.587.3808

Represented by
Suzanne Craig
918.749.9424

**Architectural Clients
Include**

CDFM
Kansas City, MO

**Frankfurt Short &
Bruza Associates**
Oklahoma City

HTB, Inc.
Oklahoma City

MATRIX
Tulsa, OK

**Page Zebrowski
Architects**
Tulsa, OK

Selected Projects

1. Emergency Medical
Services Authority
Tulsa, OK
Architect:
Fritz / Baily Architects
Tulsa, OK

2. Warren Place
Metropolitan Life
Insurance Company
Tulsa, OK
Architect:
**Thompson Ventulett,
Stainback & Associates**
Atlanta

3. AMOCO Master
Earth Station
Tulsa, OK
Architect:
Murray Jones Murray
Tulsa, OK

1

2

3

Over 20 years of providing
photography services to
architecture, interior
design, and development
firms in the Southwest.

Degree: BA in
Architectural Design,
Oklahoma State University

Member: American
Society of Magazine
Photographers.

■ Jennie Jones, Inc.

Jennie Jones, Inc.
One Cleveland Center
Suite 2900
1375 East Ninth Street
Cleveland / Ohio
44114

216.861.3850
216.861.4515 Fax

Specializing in architectural photography, including interiors, exteriors, models, construction progress photography, and full HABS/HAER documentation for the National Park Service.

Selected Project

Music & Communications
Building
Cleveland State University
Cleveland, OH
Client:
**Van Dijk, Johnson &
Partners**
Cleveland, OH

■ Sam Gray

Sam Gray Photography
23 Westwood Road
Wellesley /
Massachusetts
02181

617.237.2711

Portfolio available for a
personal presentation.

■ InSite

Glenn Cormier
828 K Street #305
San Diego / California
92101

619.237.5006
619.231.6624 Fax

Peter Malinowski
PO Box 20264
Santa Barbara / California

805.962.3870
805.962.6202 Fax

A complete list of
magazine, architectural,
and interior design clients
is available on request.

Call or fax your request for
an 8-page color brochure
showing recent work.

Member: American Society
of Magazine Photographers

Selected Projects

1,2. Hyatt Regency
at Aventine
La Jolla, CA
Architect:
Michael Graves
Princeton, NJ

3. Siegal Residence
Boca Raton, FL
Architect:
Barry Berkus
Santa Barbara, CA

4. Landsberg Residence
Temecula, CA
Architect:
Ken Kellog
San Diego, CA

1

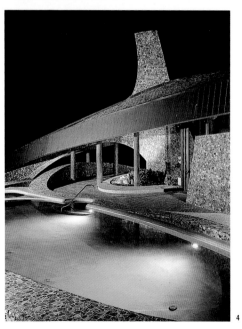

3

2

4

■ Brian R. Tolbert / Kirk Zutell

brt Photographic
Illustrations
911 State Street
Lancaster / Pennsylvania
17603

717.393.0918
717.393.1560 Fax

Photography for
architectural, interior
design, and product
installation projects
across the country.
Complete set construction
and design capabilities,
with 20 years of
experience to keep even
the largest projects
trouble free.

Clients Include

American Olean Tile

Armstrong World
Industries

Beachly Furniture

Chi-Chi's

Cole Office Environments

Columbus Coated Fabrics

Dupont Carpet Fibers

Eastman Kodak Company

Hilton Hotels

Holiday Inns

ICI Americas

JG Furniture Systems

McDonald Products

Pennsylvania House

Roffman Associates

William Sklaroff Design

Tarkett

Wood-Mode

York Wallcoverings

Please call to receive a
portfolio and a selection
of tear sheets.

■ Brian R. Tolbert / Kirk Zutell

brt Photographic
Illustrations
911 State Street
Lancaster / Pennsylvania
17603

717.393.0918
717.393.1560 Fax

Awards

Art Directions Magazine
Creativity Award

New York Art Directors'
Club Award

Philadelphia Art Directors'
Club Award

Eastman Kodak Epcot
Center Award

Best of Show
Professional Photographers
of America Art Directors'
Choice Awards

Please call to receive a
portfolio and a selection
of tear sheets.

■ Alex Atevich

Atevich Studios
325 North Hoyne Avenue
Chicago / Illinois
60612

312.942.1453
312.942.1455 Fax

Services Include

Full service studio facility

Scenic carpentry shop

Staff set designer

Provides location and studio photography for architects, interior designers, developers, general contractors, and manufacturers of construction-related products.

Extensive experience within the construction industry since 1972.

■ John C. Jenkins

Image Source, Inc.
1900 N. Tatnall Street
Wilmington / Delaware
19802

302.658.5897
302.658.5173 Fax

Architectural Clients Include

Curtis Cox Kennerly
Philadelphia

Edward D. Stone Jr. & Associates
Fort Lauderdale, FL

Ewing, Cole, Cherry, Parsky
Philadelphia

Homsey, Victorine & Samuel, Inc.
Wilmington, DE

The Kling Lindquist Partnership
Philadelphia

Moeckel Carbonell Associates, Inc.
Wilmington, DE

Simpers & Haupt Associates, Inc.
Wilmington, DE

Tetra Tech Richardson
Newark, DE

Ueland Junker McCauley
Philadelphia

Other Clients Include

Columbia Gas System, Inc.

Cushman & Wakefield

Du Pont Company

Falcon Steel

W.L. Gore Associates

Hercules, Inc.

Hilton Hotels

ICI Americas

JMB Properties

The Linpro Company

Radisson Hotels

Trammell Crow Company

The Whiting Turner Company

Winterthur Museum

Producing graphic solutions through unique composition and lighting for designs of any scale or function.

■ Scott Miles

Landmark Photography
14 Mill Stream Road
Stamford / Connecticut
06903

203.968.2696

Architectural photography
skillfully produced to
communicate the talents
of the design team.

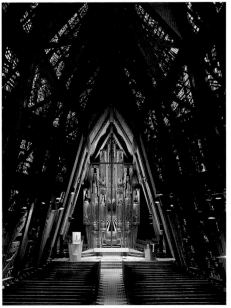

■ Richard Dale McClain

Richard Dale McClain
2212 South West Temple
Suite 6
Salt Lake City / Utah
84115

801.487.2112
800.728.9656 Toll Free

Committed to photographic artistry using careful lighting, attention to detail, and carefully chosen perspective to capture the essence of interiors and exteriors for architects, interior designers, and contractors.

Architectural Clients Include

FFKR
Salt Lake City, UT

Mediplex Medical Building Corporation
Dallas

Brixen & Christopher
Salt Lake City, UT

Niels Valentiner Associates
Salt Lake City, UT

Martin / Martin
Salt Lake City, UT

Pasker Gould Ames Weaver
Salt Lake City, UT

Jacobsen Construction
Salt Lake City, UT

Member: American Society of Magazine Photographers

■ Alise O'Brien

Alise O'Brien
6995 Washington Avenue
St. Louis / Missouri
63130

314.721.0285
314.997.6848 Fax

Publications

Commercial Renovation

Contract Design

Designers West

House Beautiful

Lighting Dimensions

Modern Healthcare

Professional Builder

Progressive Architecture

Restaurant / Hotel
Design International

**Architectural Clients
Include**

**The Christner
Partnership, Inc.**
St. Louis

Leo A. Daly Company
St. Louis

**Graham Gund
Architects**
Cambridge, MA

**Hellmuth, Obata &
Kassabaum**
St. Louis

Interior Space Inc.
St. Louis

**Stone, Marraccini, &
Patterson**
St. Louis

Team Four, Inc.
St. Louis

**The Wischmeyer
Architects**
St. Louis

Yarger Associates, Inc.
St. Louis

Selected Project

Saint Louis Galleria
Architect:
**Hellmuth, Obata &
Kassabaum**
St. Louis

■ Paul D'Innocenzo

D'Innocenzo Studios Ltd.
568 Broadway
Suite 604
New York / New York
10012

212.925.9622

To view additional work,
please refer to:
A/DC 1, page 210
A/DC 2, page 236

Member: American
Society of Magazine
Photographers; Advertising
Photographers of America

■ David Franzen

Franzen Photography
746 Ilaniwai Street
Suite 200
Honolulu / Hawaii
96813

808.537.9921
808.528.2250 Fax

Servicing the architectural, construction, and corporate markets for over 18 years.

Published extensively both nationally and internationally.

Architectural Clients Include

Kajima Associates
Los Angeles

Bechtel International
San Francisco

HKS Inc.
Dallas

Fletcher Pacific
Honolulu, HI

Ellerbe Becket
Santa Monica, CA

AIA Journal
Washington, DC

McConnell Dowell
Auckland, New Zealand

Wimberly, Allison, Tong & Goo
Honolulu, HI

Selected Project

Hawaii Prince Hotel
Honolulu, HI
Architect:
Ellerbe Becket
Santa Monica, CA

■ M. Lewis Kennedy, Jr.

M. Lewis Kennedy, Jr.
2700 Seventh Avenue South
Le Partenaire Creative
Facility
Birmingham / Alabama
35233

205.252.2700
205.252.2701 Fax

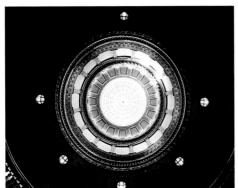

Distinctive images for architects, designers, builders, manufacturers, and publications.

Extensive location shooting cababilities. Modern studio with staff and in-house processing labs.

Portfolio and client list are available on request.

Member: American Society of Magazine Photographers; Society for Marketing Professional Services; and American Institute of Graphic Artists.

■ Matt Wargo

Matt Wargo
4236 Main Street
Philadelphia /
Pennsylvania
19127
215.483.1211
215.483.9350 Fax

Publications

Architecture

Architectural Record

Architectural Digest

Casabella

Contract

Interior Design

Interior

Progressive Architecture

A+U

Architectural Design

Design Specifier

Architectural Clients Include

The Hillier Group
Princeton, NJ

Zeidler Roberts Partnership
Toronto

The Kling-Lindquist Partnership
Philadelphia

KPA Design Group
Philadelphia

Payette Associates
Boston

International Design Group
Toronto

RTKL Associatate
Fort Lauderdale, FL

Venturi, Scott Brown Associates
Philadelphia

John Blatteau Associates
Philadelphia

Bohlin Powell Larkin Cywinski
Philadelphia

Vitetta Group
Philadelphia

■ Mardan Photography

Mardan Photography
6201 N. Winthrop Avenue
PO Box 20574
Indianapolis / Indiana
46220

317.251.8373
317.251.0629 Fax

Selected Projects

1. Private Residence
Indianapolis, IN
Developer:
Sweet & Company, Inc.
Indianapolis

2. The Ritz-Carlton
Manalapan, FL
Developer:
Centaur Consulting, Inc
Indianapolis

3. The Ritz-Carlton
Manalapan, FL
Client:
**Midwest
Woodworking, Inc**.
Indianapolis

1

2

3

Clients Include

**American Consulting
Engineers**
Indianapolis

CSO/Architects, Inc.
Indianapolis

Duke Associates
Indianapolis

Dynamic Design
Scottsdale, AZ

Eden Design Associates
Indianapolis

**F.A. Wilhelm
Construction Co. Inc.**
Indianapolis

**General Growth Center
Companies, Inc.**
Minneapolis, MN

**Howard Needles
Tammen & Bergendoff**
Indianapolis

Huber Hunt & Nichols
Indianapolis

**Shiel Sexton
Company, Inc.**
Indianapolis

**The Odle, McGuire &
Shook Coporation**
Indianapolis

Member: American
Society of Magazine
Photographers

Affiliate Member:
American Institute of
Architects, Indianapolis
Chapter

■ Cathy Kelly

CK Architectural
Photography
1209 38th Street
Sacramento / California
95816

916.457.3067
916.455.9115 Fax

Clients Include

Bechtel Group Inc.
Crocker Art Museum
The Dunlavey Studio
EDM Equities
John F. Otto Inc.
SAE Continental Heller
SD Deacon

Publications

AIA Journal
Architectural Record
Architecture
Best In Neon
Builder Magazine
Comstock's Magazine
Identity
New Homes
Print
Professional Builder
Magazine
Sacramento Magazine
Tile World
US News & World Report

Selected Project

Sacramento Tower Bridge
Sesquicentennial
Lighting Consultant:
James Earl Jewell
San Francisco

(Poster available.)

■ Cathy Kelly

CK Architectural
Photography
1209 38th Street
Sacramento / California
95816

916.457.3067
916.455.9115 Fax

**Architectural Clients
Include**

Boulder Associates
Boulder, CO

**Dreyfuss & Blackford
Architects**
Sacramento, CA

**Irwin Architectural
Partnership**
Huntington Beach, CA

**Miles Treaster &
Associates ASID**
Sacramento, CA

**Nacht & Lewis
Architects**
Sacramento, CA

**Rosekrans & Broder
Architects**
San Francisco

Vitiello Associates Inc.
Sacramento, CA

Other Clients Include

Baugh Construction

McCuen Properties

Pacific Coast Building
Products

Stretchwall / Mecho
Shades

The Turner Group

Vistawall Architectural
Products

Selected Project

Sacramento Central
Library Galleria
Sacramento, CA
Architect:
**Kaplan McLaughlin
Diaz**
San Francisco

■ James Cavanaugh

Cavanaugh On-Location
PO Box 158
Tonawanda / New York
14151-0158

716.838.8018
716.838.8022 Fax

Call to receive an original
limited edition photograph
from our portfolio.

Interior, exterior, and
aerial photography for
architects, interior
designers, engineers, and
builders.

Member: American
Society of Magazine
Photographers

Affiliate Member:
American Institute of
Architects (Buffalo, NY
Chapter)

■ Rob Fraser

Rob Fraser
211 Thompson Street
New York / New York
10012

212.677.4589
800.622.2397 Toll Free

Portfolio available upon
request.

Selected Project

World Trade Center
Port Authority of New York

As we move about our
cities and turn a corner or
glance upward, we may
catch a glimpse of a
particular building. We
create and observe new
visual relationships to
buildings depending on
where we stand or move.
Casual in nature, these
relationships are
important in the way we
relate to our architecture.

This project involved
extensive exploration, as
the World Trade Center is
never far from sight in
New York City.

■ Colin McRae

Colin McRae
1061 Folsom Street
San Francisco / California
94103

415.863.0119
415.558.0485 Fax

Publications

Architectural Record

Architecture

Business Week

Communication Arts

Designers West

Home Magazine

House & Garden

Interior Design

Interiors

Metropolitan Home

Newsweek

Progressive
Architecture

Time

■ Colin McRae

Colin McRae
1061 Folsom Street
San Francisco / California
94103

415.863.0119
415.558.0485 Fax

Clients Include

Esherick Homsey
Dodge & Davis

Gensler & Associates

Hellmuth Obata &
Kassabaum

Holland East & Duvivier

Holt Hinshaw Pfau Jones

Kaplan McLaughlin & Diaz

STUDIOS Architecture

Whisler-Patri

Ahmanson Development
Company

Apple Computer

BankAmerica Corporation

Bramalea Pacific

Campeau Development
Company

Dupont

Eastman Kodak Company

Prudential

US Air

Wells Fargo Bank

Stan Koslow

Architectural Specialty
Studios
PO Box 8426
Woodland / California
95695

916.666.3342

Conveys the architectural
concept through creative
documentation of the
structure's design and
material components.
Images exhibit a
sensitivity to the interplay
of light, color, and space
while using a distinctly
coherent and dynamic
fashion, drawing attention
to the design's vitality and
detail.

Specializes in architectural
photography, both exterior
and interior.

Traveling portfolio
available upon request.

Clients Include

Alcobond Inc.

Anshen & Allen

Benning Design

Cable Lease

Chadsworth Inc.

Clock Tower Design

Home Federal

Monighan & Associates

Nacht & Lewis

Nichols / Melburg /
Rossetto

NIIYA / Calpo /
Hom / Dong, Inc.

Stephen J. Short &
Associates

Tower of Records

US Computer Service

Williams & Paddon

■ Randall Perry

Randall Perry Photography
92 Hansen Road
Schaghticoke Hills /
New York
12154

518.664.2821
800.832.5739 Toll-Free
518.664.5122 Fax

Photographer of building interiors and exteriors for architects and interior design firms.

Widely recognized in the Northeast as a specialist in architectural photography.

Work used in advertising and corporate marketing communications materials, and featured in many national, regional, and local publications.

Member: American Institute of Architects

Architectural Clients Include

Jim Barnes Baker Associates
New York City

Edward Larabee Barnes, John M.Y. Lee
New York City

Crandall Associates
Glens Falls, NY

Crozier Associates
Albany, NY

Einhorn, Yaffee, Prescott
Albany, NY

Petersen, Ryan, Mallin, Mendle
Albany, NY

Robert Carl Williams
Pittsfield, VT

■ Barbara White

Barbara White /
Architectural Photography
712 Emerald Bay
Laguna Beach / California
92651

714-494-2479
800.237.2479 Toll Free

826 East Florida Avenue
Suite G-6
Denver / Colorado
80231

Patience to arrange for the optimum lighting. Insight to frame from the perfect perspective. Clarity of vision to extract the essence of a setting.

Portfolio and client list available on request.

Publications

American Photographer

Architectural Record

Audio / Video Interiors

Business Interiors

Designer Specifier

Designers West

Interior Sources

Laguna

Orange Coast

Orange County

Professional Builder

Southern California
Home & Garden

South Coast

Sun Coast
Architect/Builder

Selected Project

Prime Ticket Network
Los Angeles
Interior Designer:
**Andrew Gerhard
Interiors, Ltd.**
Rancho La Costa, CA

■ Beth Singer

Beth Singer Photographer,
Inc.
25741 River Drive
Franklin / Michigan
48025

313.626.4860
313.932.3496 Fax

Clients Include

Des Rosiers Architects,
Inc.

General Motors
Corporation
(Argonaut AEC)

Ghafari Associates, Inc.

Giffels Associates, Inc.

Greiner, Inc.

Harley Ellington Pierce
Yee Associates, Inc.

Howard, Needles,
Tammen & Bergendoff

Albert Kahn Associates

Masco Corporation

Prudential Property Co.

Victor Saroki Associates

Sikes, Jennings & Kelley

Robert A. M. Stern

Sub-Zero Freezer Company

Publications

AIA Place

Architectural Record

Athletic Business

Better Homes & Gardens

Builder

Builders Design &
Construction

Business Facilities

Commercial Renovation

Contract Magazine

Designer Magazine

Detroit Monthly

Fine Homes

Kitchen & Bath Business

Professional Builder

The Quarton Group

Tokyo Business

Member: ASMP and SMPS

Affiliate Member: AIA,
Detroit Chapter

■ Thomas K. Leighton

321 East 43rd Street
Penthouse 12
New York / New York
10017

212.370.1835

Architectural, interior, and
structural photography
with a special empnasis
on color and graphics.

For additional images, see
A/DC 1 and 2.

Client list, portfolio, and
stock photography
available upon request.

■ Thomas K. Leighton

321 East 43rd Street
Penthouse 12
New York / New York
10017

212.370.1835

Architectural, interior, and
structural photography
with a special emphasis
on color and graphics.

For additional images, see
A/DC 1 and 2.

Client list, portfolio, and
stock photography
available upon request.

■ David Plank

Plank Photography
Cherry & Carpenter Streets
Reading / Pennsylvania
19602

215.376.3461
215.376.8261 Fax

Licensed, instrument-rated pilot. Company plane.

Fifteen years of experience photographing residential, commercial, and industrial interiors and exteriors.

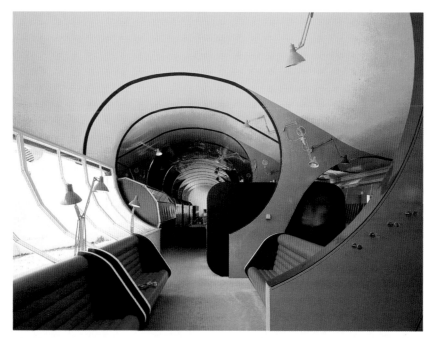

■ Russell Abraham Photography

Russell Abraham
60 Federal Street
Suite 303
San Francisco / California
94107

415.896.6400
415.896.6402 Fax

Publications

Architectural Digest
Architectural Record
Architecture
Designers West
Interiors
Interior Design
Progressive Architecture
Restaurant & Hotel
Design International

**Architectural Clients
Include**

**Daniel Mann Johnson
Mendenhall**
Los Angeles
San Francisco

**Hellmuth Obata
Kassabaum**
San Francisco
St. Louis, MO

Interior Architects
San Francisco
Los Angeles

Leo A. Daly, Intl.
Omaha, NE

Rosser / FABRAP
Atlanta

Roche Dinkeloo
Hamden, CT

**Robinson Mills &
Williams**
San Francisco

Swatt Architects
San Francisco

Takenaka, Intl.
San Francisco
Tokyo

**Walker Warner
Architects**
San Francisco

Member: American
Institute of Architects;
American Society of
Magazine Photographers

Degrees in architecture
and design from
University of California
at Berkeley

■ Paul E. Burd

Paul E. Burd Photography
300 East Hydraulic Street
Yorkville / Illinois
60560

708.553.7510

Publications

Chicago Magazine
Estate Magazine
Country Home Magazine
Popular Mechanics
Specifying Engineer

Commercial and editorial
photography with an
emphasis on dramatic
lighting and a strong
sense of design.

■ Campbell & Kamphaus

C & K Photographics
Philip Grussenmeyer
Stephen Pyle
Rural Route 8
Box 95
Union School Road
Decatur / Illinois
62522

800.777.8188 Toll Free
217.963.2135 Fax

Photography of interiors, exteriors, and models for architects, developers, and designers. Specializing in publication, advertising, and documentation.

Member: Professional Photographers of America ("Q" rating); American Society of Magazine Photographers; and the American Institute of Architects (Central Illinois Chapter)

Clients Include

BLDD Architects

LZT & Associates

Philip Swager & Associates

Henneman Raufiesen

Architectural Spectrum

Christner Partnership

Battielle Corporation

Caterpillar

Corn Products Company

Tate & Lyle

Bunn Corporation

Archer Daniels Midland

Construx of Illinois

Ultimate Interiors

Hilton Hotels
(Los Angeles)

Awards

Illinois Photographer of the Year 1991

Illinois Commercial Photographer of the Year 1989, 1991

Kodak International Gallery Award Recipient 1985, 1989, 1990, 1991

Epcot Gallery Exhibition 1985, 1989, 1990, 1991

■ Mel Curtis

Mel Curtis
2400 East Lynn Street
Seattle / Washington
98112

206.323.1230

Represented by
Donna Jorgensen
Annie Barrett, Associate
206.634.1880

Portfolio available upon
request.

See A/DC 2 for additional
work.

■ Mert Carpenter

Mert Carpenter
Photography
202 Granada Way
Los Gatos / California
95030

408.370.1663
408.370.1668 Fax

Graphic, dramatic, and creative photography for architects and the building industry for over 15 years.

Architectural Clients Include

Field Paoli Architects
San Francisco

Koll Construction
Pleasanton, CA

DES Architects
Redwood City, CA

San Jose Redevelopment Agency
San Jose, CA

Rick Guidice Architect
Los Gatos, CA

Ruth & Going Architects
San Jose, CA

Karen Butera Inc. Interiors
Palo Alto, CA

Provident Development
Austin, TX

The Grupe Company
Stockton, CA

Hathaway Construction
San Jose, CA

■ John Gillan

John Gillan
Photography, Inc.
12168 SW 131st Avenue
Miami / Florida
33186

305.251.4784
305.388.2255 Fax

Selected Projects

1. Physics Building
University of Miami
Miami
Architect:
**Spillis Candela &
Partners, Inc.**
Coral Gables, FL

2. Offices of Zuckerman
Staeder Taylor & Evans
Miami
Interior Designer:
**Joyce / Snoweiss
Design Group**
Coconut Grove, FL

3. Pier 66 Resort
Fort Lauderdale, FL
Interior Designer:
Dawn Starling
Miami

1

2

3

Architectural Clients Include

**Sandy & Babcock
Architects Planners**
San Francisco
Miami

**The Richie
Organization**
Boston
Sarasota, FL

**Chen & Associates
Incorporated**
Miami

**The Smith, Korach,
Hayet, Haynie
Partnership**
Miami

**The Nichols
Partnership Inc.**
Coral Gables, FL

Camar Graniti, SPA
Rome, Italy

The Prudential
Coral Gables, FL

Member: American
Society of Magazine
Photographers; Board of
Directors for South Florida
Chapter

■ Dan Ham

Dan Ham Photography
1350 Manufacturing #212
Dallas / Texas 75207

214.742.8700
214.638.1905 Fax

317 Burch Street
Box 6421
Taos / New Mexico 87571

505.751.0602
505.751.0602 Fax

■ Jeffrey Jacobs

Mims Studios
2258 Young Avenue
Memphis / Tennessee
38104

901.725.4040
901.725.7643 Fax

Selected Projects

1. Fulton County
Government Center
Atlanta
Architects:
Turner / FABRAP
Joint Venture
Atlanta

Publications

Architecture
Better Homes & Gardens
Builder Magazine
Decorating & Remodeling
House & Garden
Interior Construction
Professional Photographer

1

Dedicated to the artful
expression of architectural
form in photography.
Technical excellence with
attention to critical detail.
Reliable. Professional.

For additional images,
see A/DC 2.

Jeffrey Jacobs

Mims Studios
2258 Young Avenue
Memphis / Tennessee
38104

901.725.4040
901.725.7643 Fax

Clients Include

Holiday Inn World Wide

Trammell Crow

Federal Express

Turner Construction

Equity Group Investments

Boyle Investment Company

Koger Properties

Archer / Malmo
Advertising

Windsor Properties

Selected Projects

2. Archer / Malmo
Advertising
Memphis
Architect:
**Looney, Ricks, Kiss
Architects**
Memphis

3. Children's Museum
of Memphis
Memphis
Exhibit Design:
Williamson / Haizlip
Memphis

2

3

For additional images,
see A/DC 2.

■ Rick Taylor

Taylor Photography
1850 Alderbrook Road
PO Box 29745
Atlanta / Georgia
30359

404.634.8333

Clients Include

Allied Fibers

Anderson Windows

AT&T

Atlanta Journal
Constitution

Better Homes & Gardens

Blue Cross Blue Shield

Bruce Hardwood Floors

Convalescent Services Inc.

Country America

Country Home

Digital Equipment Corp.

Economy Forms Corp.

Kimberly Clark

Meredith Special Interest

Milliken Research Corp.

Professional Builder

Southern Accents

Southern Bell

Sumner Rider & Associates

Traditional Home

Selected Projects

1. Electric Smart House
Stone Mountain, GA
Client:
**Sumner Rider &
Associates**
Washington, DC

2. Georgia Dome
Atlanta, GA
Client:
**Economy Forms
Corporation**
Des Moines, IA

1

2

Photography for
advertising, architecture,
brochures, and
publications.

Portfolio available on
request.

■ Maxwell MacKenzie

Maxwell MacKenzie
2641 Garfield Street NW
Washington / DC
20008

202.232.6686

Publications

Abitare

Architecture

Architectural Record

Better Homes & Garden

Business Interiors

Historic Preservation

Home

Interior Design

Interiors

Landscape Architecture

Professional Office Design

Progressive Architecture

Restaurant Business

Time-Life Books

Travel & Leisure

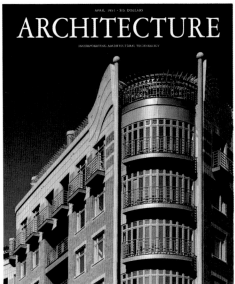

Architectural Clients Include

Adamstein & Demetriou
Washington, DC

Brennan Beer Gorman
New York City

Burroughs Roos Grierson
Washington, DC

Deupi & Associates
Washington, DC

Joseph Boggs Studio
Washington, DC

Keyes Condon Florance Eichbaum Esocoff King
Washington, DC

KressCox Associates
Washington, DC

Leo A. Daly
Omaha, NE

Oldham & Seltz
Washington, DC

RTKL Associates
Baltimore

Sasaki Associates
Watertown, MA

Studios
Washington, DC

Weinstein Associates
Washington, DC

Other Clients Include

Greycoat

Homart

Melvin Simon

Metropolitan Life

Mobil

■ Bob Swanson

Swanson Images
532 Lisbon Street
San Francisco / California
94112

415.585.6567

"The Ariaga House –
Majesty in Ruins", from the
book *Home Sweet Jerome*
(Jerome Headlands Press,
in progress), about the
National Historic Landmark
town of Jerome, Arizona.

"A minor theme through
all the stories told me
were their definitions of
Jerome, epitaphs etched
into their memories, like
the names on the
tombstones just outside of
town surrounded by
wrought iron cages that
kept coyotes from digging
up the graves."

Diane Rappaport
Home Sweet Jerome

■ Bob Swanson

Swanson Images
532 Lisbon Street
San Francisco / California
94112

415.585.6567

Publications

Architectural Record

Interiors

Designers West

Visual Merchandising &
Store Design

Architectural Lighting

Engineering News Record

Sound & Video Contractor

**Architectural Clients
Include**

**Robinson Mills &
Williams**
San Francisco

Backen Arrigoni & Ross
San Francisco

Erlich Rominger
Mountain View, CA

George Famous / AT&T
San Leandro, CA

Gensler & Associates
San Francisco

**Daniel Mann Johnson &
Menderhall**
San Francisco

**Plant Construction
Company**
San Francisco

Rudolph & Sletten
Foster City, CA

Bedford Properties
San Francisco

Bold design statements
created through attention
to detail, structural
composition and nearly four
decades of photographic
and building industry
experience.

■ Kevin C. Rose

Rose Studio, Inc.
146 Walker Street
Atlanta / Georgia
30313

404.521.0729
404.521.0708 Fax

Clients Include

American Standard

AT&T

Chapman, Coyle,
Chapman, Powell
Interiors

Coca-Cola

Crystal Marble

DuPont / Corian

Harbinger Carpet

Lucite Paint

Macy's

Niles Bolton &
Associates

Rosser FABRAP
International

Salem Carpet Mills

Taylor & Mathis

Thompson, Ventulett,
Stainback & Associates

Trammell Crow Company

Publications

Architectural Digest

Better Homes & Gardens

Contract

Designers West

Elle Decor

Interior Design

Interiors

Kitchen & Bath Ideas

Progressive Architecture

Southern Accents

Southern Homes

Veranda

Victorian Homes

Specializing in "architectural
advertising," giving that
dramatic look to your
interiors, exteriors, and
architectural products.

Styling and production
services available.

■ George Cott

Chroma, Inc.
2802 Azeele Street
Tampa / Florida
33609

813.873.1374
813.871.3448 Fax

Architectural photography with a sensitivity for the design and lighting of exterior and interior spaces.

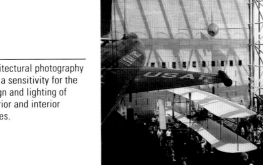

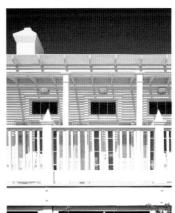

Architectural Clients Include

Hellmuth, Obata & Kassabaum
St. Louis, MO
Tampa, FL
Washington, DC

Jung Brannen Associates
Boston

The Architects Collaborative
Cambridge, MA

Associated Space Design
Tampa, FL
Washington, DC

Hansen Lind Meyer
Orlando, FL

Rowe Holmes Hammer Russell
Tampa, FL

Cooper Johnson Smith Architects
Tampa, FL

HKS
Dallas

Swanke Hayden Connell
New York City

Michael Shepperd
Sarasota, FL

■ Marco P. Zecchin

Image Center
Photographic Design
1219 Willo Mar Drive
San Jose / California
95118

408.723.3649

Architectural and interior
design photography
conveying the
professional's vision.

Publications

Builders & Contractor

Home

Home Ideas

House Beautiful

Northern California Home
& Gardens

Northwest Kitchens & Bath

Palo Alto Times
Home Magazine

Panorama / Italy

Professional Builder

Sweet's

■ Shields-Marley

Shields-Marley
Photography
117 South Victory Street
Little Rock / Arkansas
72201-1827

501.372.6148
501.374.2111 Fax

Selected Projects

1. University of Arkansas
at Fayetteville
Old Main Renovation
Architect:
**Mott Mobley McGowan
& Griffin**
Fort Smith, AR

2. Leisure Arts, Inc.
Architect:
**Brooks Jackson
Architects**
Little Rock, AR

Awards

AIA Design Awards
1987, 1988, 1989,1991

ADDY Award
1990, 1991

United States Air Force
Design Awards
1990, 1991

Arkansas Times
Interior Design Awards
1988, 1989, 1990

IABC Excellence in
Communications
1986, 1987, 1988

PRSA Prism Awards
1986

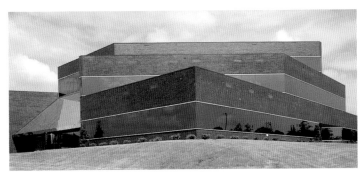

Blending photographic
technique with visual
ingenuity to capture the
art of the designer, on
location or in the studio.
See A/DC 2 for additional
work or call for a portfolio.

■ Gary Hofheimer Photography

Gary Hofheimer
59-052 Huelo Street
Haleiwa / Hawaii
96712

808.638.9092
808.638.8847 Fax

Honolulu-based
photography business
in second decade of
service for clients'
advertising, corporate,
and editorial needs.

Member: American
Society of Magazine
Photographers

Clients Include

Transpacific Development
Corporation

Coldwell Banker
Commercial

Hilton Hotels

Hyatt Hotels

Hemmeter Corporation

Myers Corporation

Bank of Hawaii

Regency Group

Asahi Jyuken, USA

Ohbayashi Corporation

Mitsui Rehouse Realty

Kumagai Gumi Co., Ltd.

Haseko USA

Japan Travel Bureau

The Lodge at Koele
Island of Lana'i, Hawaii
Developer:
**Castle & Cooke
Properties**
Honolulu, HI

■ HELIOSTUDIO

William H. Kloubec
PO Box 3744
Minneapolis / Minnesota
55403

612.377.0648

PO Box 1008
New York / New York
10013

212.674.0725

Providing advanced
architectural, commercial,
corporate, hotel,
industrial, property,
restaurant, and scientific
photographic services in
the US and worldwide.

Selected Projects

1. Restaurant Interior
Pizzeria Uno Corporation
Baltimore Harbor, MD

2. La Mirage
Albuquerque, NM
Developer:
**Trammell Crow
Company**
Phoenix

3. Private Residence
Minneapolis, MN
Architect:
Tom Gunkelman
Minneapolis, MN

■ Douglas Peebles

Douglas Peebles
445 Iliwahi Loop
Kailua / Hawaii
96734

808.254.1082
808.254.1267 Fax

Specializing in interior and exterior architectural photography with an eye towards the architect's use of lighting.

All formats 4x5 to 35mm. Large selection of aerial photographs of Hawaii available.

Member: American Society of Magazine Photographers

■ Ken Bryan

Ken Bryan
PO Box 1977
Harvard Square
Cambridge /
Massachusetts
02238

617.868.2323

Selected Projects

1. *Harmony*
58" x 70" x 5"

2. *Rhapsody*
58" x 70" x 5"

Light-reflective sculptures that show the ever-changing colors of the spectrum on high tech materials.

Spectra-Wall Sculptures require atrium or skylit room placement with natural or artificial light from above and can be created in any size.

These light-reflective, high tech sculptures are owned by many private collectors in the entertainment, medical, and business professions.

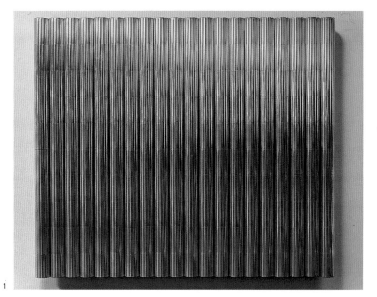

1

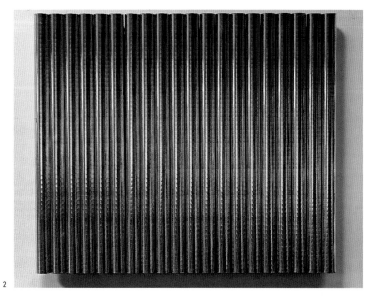

2

Publications

Art in America

ARTFORUM

ARTnews

ARTSPACE

Sculpture

■ George Greenamyer

George M. Greenamyer
Careswell Sculpture &
Iron Works
994 Careswell Street
Marshfield / Massachusetts
02050

617.834.9688

Creates site-specific outdoor public sculptures that often function as physical and narrative gateways.

Designs a visual narrative using historical or contemporary references including local idiosyncracies, legends, and architecture.

Consults with wind, structural, and electrical engineers and lighting designers to create wind machines and internally lit sculptures.

Selected Projects

Germantown 1920, 1991
Internally Lit Gateway
22' x 13' x 3'
forged, fabricated, &
painted steel
Up County Government
Center
Montgomery County Art
in Architecture
Germantown, MD

University of Oregon
Eugene, OR

Iowa State University
Ames, IA

University of Alaska
Fairbanks, AK

Caroline Freeland Park
Bethesda, MD

University of Wisconsin
Milwaukee, WI

Public Safety Building
Wilmington, DE

Lechmere Parking Garage
Cambridge, MA

Dadeland Transit Station
Miami, FL

American Electric Power
Columbus, OH

Photo Credit
Beverly Burbank

Services Include

Design

Drafting

Fabrication

Blacksmithing

Painting

Site Preparation

Installation

Photography

■ Karen Petersen

Karen A. Petersen,
Sculptor
Chase Hill Road
PO Box 1
Abington / Connecticut
06230

203.974.3330

Stylized animals, figures, and fantasy creatures in bronze and other weather-resistant materials.

Sculptures appropriate for parks, courtyards, lobbies, small interior spaces, and wherever fine sculpture is welcome.

Work commissioned for both private and corporate collections.

Member: Sculptor Society of Canada

Commisions Include

Dobson Associates
Westfield Nursing Home
Westfield, MA

The Sard Corporation
West Hartford, CT

Hartford College for Women
Hartford, CT

Landev Corporation
Simsbury, CT

Chamber of Commerce
Hartford, CT

Cynthia & Leo O. Harris
Hampton, CT

■ Jon Barlow Hudson

Jon Barlow Hudson
PO Box 710
Studio: 325 N Walnut Street
Yellow Springs / Ohio
45387

513.767.7766
513.767.7766 Auto / Fax

Selected Projects

Fenestrae Aeternitatis:
Windows Into Infinity
painted 410 stainless steel
7'h x 3'd x 16'l
propose 12'h stainless
steel

Morning Star
mirrored stainless steel
World Expo '88
Creative Director:
John Truscott
Melbourne, Australia

Triskelion Continuum
painted steel
12' diameter
Federal Mogul
Lititz, PA
Architect:
Giffles
Southfield, MI

Ts'ung Music
brass & stainless steel
9 units; 3' – 27'h
PDT Architects &
Planners
Cincinnati, OH

Architectural Clients
Include

Mulia Tower
Jakarta, Indonesia
Architect:
ARC PAC
Hong Kong
Jakarta

Eppley Field Airport
Omaha, NE
Architect:
Dana Larson Roubel
Omaha, NE

South Regional
Courthouse
Hollywood, FL
Art in Public Spaces
E.F. Saar
Ft. Lauderdale, FL

Warner / Lambert Corp.
Morris Plains, NJ
Architect:
Ewing Cole Cherry &
Parsky
Philadelphia, PA

National Radio Astronomy
Observatory
Socorro, NM
Architect:
Mallery Stevens
Campbell & Pearl
Albuquerque, NM

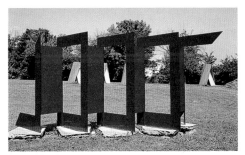

Sculpture for any
architectural situation.
Sizes range from 1 to 30
meters or higher.

Sculptures made from
stainless steel and other
metals; cast bronze; or
stone, water, and light.

Available for projects
worldwide. Inquiries
welcomed.

■ Venice Neon Company

Venice Neon Company
Michael Cohen
Connie Wexler Cohen
1221 Abbot Kinney Blvd.
Venice / California
90291

310.392.4041
310.314.4810 Fax

Specializing in innovative,
site-specific design and
project management for
large-scale neon and
mixed-media installations,
at both private and public
locations.

Member: Design
Lighting Forum

Clients Include

Minnesota NBA
Association

Arical Properties

Arthur Andersen & Company

Adams Publishing, Inc.

International Interiors, Inc.

Radisson Hotel

Clarion Hotel

Avnery Development

Photo Credits

Shin Koyama

Connie Cohen

Publications

Architectural Record
Lighting

Lighting Dimensions

Signs of the Times

■ Rob Fisher

Environmental Sculpture
228 N Allegheny Street
Bellefonte / Pennsylvania
16823

814.355.1458
814.231.1344 Fax

Clients Include

Ball-Unimark Corporation

Carnegie Science Center

Carolina Corporate Center

City of Hamamatsu
(Japan)

DeBartolo Corporation

Gateway Science Center
(Philadelphia)

Howard Johnson Corp.

Kingdom of Saudi Arabia

Mellon Bank

New York Hilton

Osaka Hilton International
(Japan)

Playboy Corporation

Trump Corporation

Water Pollution Control
Federation

Westcor Partners (Arizona)

International lecturer on
art and technology.

Bachelor of Science in
Humanities, Engineering,
and Visual Design,
Massachusetts Institute
of Technology (1961)

Fulbright Fellowship,
University of Oslo (1962),
University of Rome (1963)

Master of Industrial
Design, Syracuse
University (1965)

Other awards include
Rockefeller Foundation
Grant (1981); Meritorious
Design, Vietnam Veterans
Memorial (1981); Special
Projects, Pennsylvania
Council on the Arts (1986,
1987, and 1989).

Featured on CNN Science
& Technology News and
USIA Worldnet television;
in Sculpture Magazine
and Leonardo Journal;
and in both national and
international exhibitions.

Co-author of *The Design
Continuum* (Van Nostrand
Reinhold, NY, 1966).

Photo Credit

Al Payne

Selected Project

Symphony of the Air
Scottsdale, AZ 1991

■ Kay Whitcomb

Enamels by Kay Whitcomb
209 South Street
Rockport / Massachusetts
01966

508.546.6930

Exhibitions Include

Internacional Esmalti
Madrid, Spain 1991

Cloisonne
Near & Far Gallery
Mill Valley, CA 1991

Angels
ArtSpace Gallery
Atlanta, GA 1991

Society of Arts & Crafts
Boston 1987, 1988, 1990

Art Council Gallery
Public Library
Port Washington, NY 1989

International Email
Coburg, West Germany
1987

Bellevue Museum of Art
Bellevue, WA 1987

San Diego Museum of Art
Solo Exhibition
1965-80, 1984, 1987

California Design
Pasadena Museum
Pasadena, CA
Shows #8, 9, & 11

International Shippo
Ueno Royal Museum
Tokyo, Japan
1978, 1979, 1981, 1985,
1989

Specializes in four enamel
techniques – enamel on
copper, porcelain enamel
on steel, champlevé, and
cloisonné objects –
applied to large wall
ornaments, architectural
wall murals, doors and
more. Designs often
include phrases set in
steel, concrete, or other
materials. Vitreous
surfaces are durable,
weather resistant, and
have a long life with low
maintenance requirements.

Honorary Degrees: Rhode
Island School of Design
Cambridge School of Art

Awards juror at Limoges,
France, 1984. Prizewinner
at Limoges, France, (1978)
and Tokyo, Japan (1981,
1984)

Works include many
private commissions.

Selected Projects

40" x 60" wall mural
Town Hall
Gosselies, Belgium

5' x 10' wall mural
University Hospital
San Diego

8' x 97' porcelan enamel
on steel mural
International Airport
Dubai, UAE

■ Jack Marshall

Levity, Ltd.
30 Coolidge Street
Keene / New Hampshire
03431

603.357.4136

Award-winning sculptor who designs and executes furniture, environmental art, creative tile and lighting fixtures, wall reliefs, and full-round sculpture.

Current "The Law of Levity" series spawned super-comfortable furniture, tiles that "pick up" their walls, lamps that "lighten" their spaces, and other sculptures, all of which defy the Earth's gravity. And all for spaces that could use a lift.

Serious attention to planning, coordination, technical research, fabrication, and installation.

Degrees: MED, Yale University School of Architecture; MFA, Boston University School of Visual Arts

Brochure; video; and awards, exhibitions, and commissions list available upon request.

Selected Projects

1. *Baroquen Premises*
(terre cotte figures in mixed-media installation)
25' x 20' x 12' area shown
Brockton Museum
Brockton, MA 1982-83
Italy (touring exhibit) 1983

2. *Senza Gravita*
("Law of Levity" Series)
30" x 14" x 14"
unique cast bronze

3. *Nine to Five*
unique cast bronze
18" x 15" x 8"

4. *Mac Hines Elegy II*
("Law of Levity" Series)
18" x 18" x 10"
unique cast aluminum

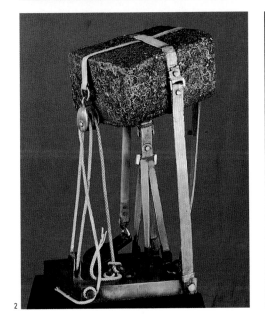

Awards

Olivetti Award for
Contemporary Sculpture

Ford Foundation
Purchase Award

■ Maryrose Carroll

Maryrose Carroll
1682 North Ada
Chicago / Illinois
60622

312.342.7282
312.248.8392 Fax

Clients Include

Sol LeWitt (artist)
Northwestern University
Inglis Art
Walter Netsch, AIA
Dayton Art Museum
Illinois State Art Museum

Selected Projects

1. *Bosk of Spring Trees*
Evanston, IL
Developer:
Rescorp, Inc.
Chicago

2. *In Dreams Begin
Responsibilities*
Chicago, IL
Developer:
Metropolitan Structures
Chicago

3. *Three Trees*
San Diego
Developer:
Daley Corporation
San Diego, CA

4. *Lincoln Tree*
Springfield, IL
Client:
State Journal Register
Springfield, IL

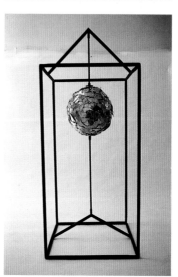

Specializing in site-specific sculptural installations that combine organic and geometric elements. Permanent installations include freestanding outdoor and indoor sculpture in lightweight aluminum.

■ Katherine Holzknecht

Katherine Holzknecht
22828 57th Avenue SE
Woodinville / Washington
98072

206.481.7788

Creates unique mixed-media artworks for architectural spaces. Site-specific art results from collaboration with design professionals to produce innovative artworks that are well suited for the location.

Projects incorporate a variety of materials from high-tech and construction sources.

Specializing in full-spectrum colors and visual textures to enhance existing design features.

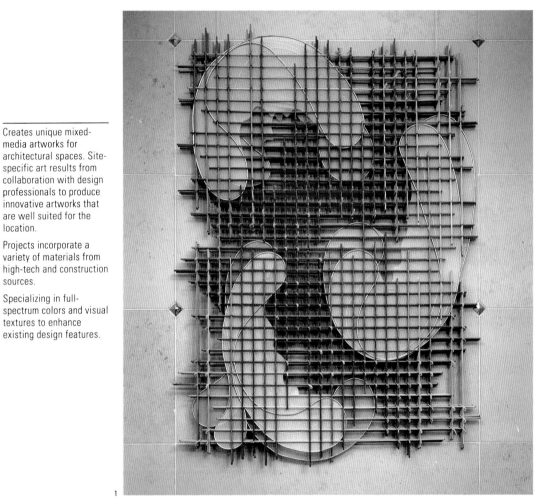

1

Selected Projects

1. Westlake Center Office Tower
Seattle
Developers:
Westlake Center Associates
Seattle
The Rouse Company
Seattle
Koehler McFayden & Company
Seattle

2. Shriners Hospital
Spokane, WA
Architects:
The NBBJ Group
Seattle
ALSC Architects
Spokane, WA
Art Agent:
Corporate Art West
Bellevue, WA

International Corporate Center at Rye, NY
Architect:
Papp Architects, PC
White Plains, NY
Developer:
The Gateside Corporation
Rye, NY

2

Photo Credit

1. Roger
   Schreiber
2. Alan Bisson

■ Barbara Shawcroft

Barbara Shawcroft
4 Anchor Drive #243
Emeryville / California
94608

510.658.6694

Selected Projects

Bay Area Rapid Transit
Architect:
**Tallie Maule, Herzka &
Knowles Associates**
Finland; USA

The Three Embarcadero
Center
Client:
**David Rockefeller &
Associates**
Architect:
John Portman
Atlanta; San Francisco

Water Resources Control
Board Building
Client:
State of California
Architect:
**Barry Wasserman &
Whitson Cox**
Sacramento, CA

Exhibitions

Sixth & Third
International Triennial
Poland

Tenth & Sixth
International Biennial
Switzerland

Americas and Japan
Tokyo, Kyoto, Japan

Museum of
Contemporary Crafts
New York City

Museum of
Contemporary Art
Chicago

Cleveland Museum
Cleveland

Third International Textile
Competition and Exhibition
Museum of Kyoto
Kyoto, Japan

Knots & Nets-Africa
North and Sub-Sahara

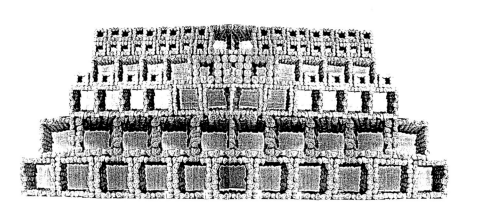

■ AZO Inc.

Susan Singleton
Andrew Shewman
1101 East Pike Street
Seattle / Washington
98122

206.322.0390
800.344.0390 Toll Free

Artist Studio
Sculpture Workshop
Print Atelier
Public Commissions
Design Collaboration
Edition Publishing
Exhibition Portfolio

Collections

The Beacon Corporation
Blue Cross / Blue Shield
The Boeing Company
Children's Hospital
Humana Corporation
The Hyatt Corporation
Maycenters
Nordstrom
Pacific Bell
Safeco Insurance Co.
Seafirst Bank
Sea-Tac Airport
Seattle City Light
UCLA Medical Center
Union Oil Corporation
University of Washington
Washington Federal
Wells Fargo
Westin Hotels
Weyerhaeuser Co.
Woodmark Hotel

Photo Credits
Kevin Latona
Rick Semple

Ziggurat (detail)
Ziggurat and artist
12' x 12'
Susan Singleton

The Messenger
8' x 7' x 4'
Andrew Shewman

■ David Floyd

David Floyd Sculpture
PO Box 490222
Key Biscayne / Florida
33149

305.532.5859
305.447.7738

Exhibitions

Art for Architects
Nina Owen, Ltd.
Chicago 1988

Floyd / Bond: New Works
Gellert Fine Arts
Miami 1988

Contemporary Artists
Phyllis Morris
Los Angeles 1989

Art in Scale
Cultural Resource Center
Miami 1990

Beyond the Ken
Miami Design Center
Miami 1991

Rediscovering the Americas
Bacardi Art Gallery
Miami 1991

Unique fountains from the *Lifesource* series, indoor and outdoor sculpture in stainless steel and water. Works may be commissioned from existing maquettes or designed for specific sites, from 8' to monumental size.

Concern for both the environment and the practical, safe operation of the fountains governs the design and engineering of each piece. All water is recirculated. Outdoor sculptures can be made to operate only when adequate rainfall has accumulated. Pumps used are lowest wattage possible; electrical equipment is ground-fault wired for safety; chemicals, if any, are as safe as those used in swimming pools.

Brochure available upon request.

Publications

ARTnews

Sculpture

Photo Credit
Steven Hlavac

■ Pamela Joseph

Pamela Joseph
Metal Paintings, Inc.
RR #3 Box 140
Pound Ridge / New York
10576

914.764.8208
914.764.8215 Fax

Other Projects

Entry Doors
Embassy of the Hungarian
People's Republic
Washington, DC
Architect:
Burns & Loewe
Scranton, PA

Contoured Panel
Piccoli Playground
1% Philadelphia Council
on the Arts
Architect:
Rothschild & Horn
Philadelphia

Iceland Spar Sculptures
Allied Services for the
Handicapped
Scranton, PA
Architect:
Palumbo & Horlacher
Scranton, PA

Elevator Lobby
Federal Courthouse
GSA Project
San Jose, CA
Architect:
**Hellmuth Obata &
Kassabaum**
San Francisco

Lobby Sculpture
Danbury Pharmacal
Carmel, NY
Architect:
Henry Loheac
Scarsdale, NY

Exhibitions

Stamford Museum &
Nature Center
Stamford, CT

Katonah Gallery
Katonah, NY

Vassar College
Art Gallery
Poughkeepsie, NY

Hudson River Museum
Yonkers, NY

Fairfield University
Fairfield, CT

Aldrich Museum of
Contemporary Art
Ridgefield, CT

Everhart Museum
Scranton, PA

Selected Project

Golden Pyramid
(commissioned window
sculptures)
Van Cleef & Arpels, Inc.
New York City
11" x 12" x 13"
stone aggregate, stacked
laminated mahogany, gold
leaf, aluminum, and lacquer

Photo Credit

Bedford
Photographic

■ Karl Rosenberg

136 North 8th Street
Brooklyn / New York
11211

718.388.8168
212.475.2515

RD #1, Box 180
Andes / New York
13731

914.586.3067

Selected Projects

AT&T Eastern
Headquarters
galleria, atrium, and
executive office pieces
Architect:
Kohn Pederson & Fox
New York City

116 Inverness
exterior, lobby, and
atrium pieces
Architect:
C. Fentress
Denver, CO

Chesapeake & Potomac
Telephone
two atrium aerials
Architect:
D. Coupard
Rockville, MD

Linclay Center III
four-story waterfall piece
Architect:
HIXON
Cincinnati, OH

Other Projects Include

Raddison Hotels
(O'Hare, Downers Grove,
and Glenview)
three atrium aerials
Walden Investment
Company
Architect:
**Skidmore, Owings &
Merrill**
Chicago

Walden Galleria,
Berkshire Galleria, and
Poughkeepsie Galleria
Malls
five atrium aerials
Pyramid Companies of
Syracuse
Architect:
DAL PAS
Syracuse, NY

Sculptor producing multi-
media, site-specific art.

See A/DC 1 and 2 for
additional projects.

■ Brian Stotesbery

Brian Stotesbery
500 Molino Street
Suite 218
Los Angeles / California
90013

213.617.7987

Exhibitions

Museum of Neon Art
Los Angeles 1992

Centennial Alumni Exhibition
College of Art & Design
Minneapolis, MN 1986

Sci-Expo
San Diego, CA 1986

An Exhibition of
Light & Logic
Coffman Gallery
Minneapolis, MN 1984

Minnesota Museum of Art
St. Paul, MN 1977

Helen Euphrate Gallery
Cupertino, CA 1977

Pavilion for the Arts
Chicago 1977

Electric Art in Boxes
The Electric Gallery
Toronto, Canada 1976

Selected Projects

Image Cube
Computer-controlled
light sculpture
IDS Center
Minneapolis, MN
Client:
Olympus Corporation
Minneapolis, MN

Ascending Cross Section
Computer-controlled
light sculpture
Private Residence
Minneapolis, MN

Neon Gears
Electronic sculpture
Client:
Marquette National Bank
Minneapolis, MN

Laser Light Sculpture
IDS Center
Minneapolis, MN
Space planner:
Jamieson & Associates, Inc.
Minneapolis, MN

Lighting for Elevator
Private Residence
Wayzata, MN

Site-specific computer
and electronically
controlled artworks for
incorporation into public
spaces, including subway
stations, theater interiors,
building exteriors, and
outdoor sculptures. Video
featuring works in motion
is available upon request.

■ Jennifer Mackey

Chia Jen Studio
PO Box 469
Scotia / California
95565

707.764.5877
707.444.6507

Specializing in fabrics for wall coverings, floor cloths, upholstery, table linens, and sculptures that often evoke a Japanese mood.

Practical and rich, the silks, cottons, and linens are also durable and easily cleaned.

Work represented in several national publications, galleries, and specialty stores.

Collaborations and private or corporate commissions welcome.

Clients Include

American Artisan

Cedanna

Findahl's

Humboldt County Cultural Center

Neiman Marcus

Society of Arts & Crafts (Boston)

Tesoro

Photo Credit
Walter Jebbe

■ Juan & Patricia Navarrete

Navarrete Studio
PO Box 2251
Taos / New Mexico
87571

505.776.2942

Interior and exterior sculpture designed to respect and complement architectural environments. Created within dictates of architectural style, site, function, engineering, and budget. Extensive background in collaborative site-specific projects from conceptual designs and fabrication to installation.

Specializing in concrete, plasters, stone, and a variety of metals that become spectacular fireplaces, grand entrances, multi-dimensional murals, and meditative fountains, exacting in detail, for corporate, residential, and public environmental settings.

Selected Projects

Central Avenue
Beautification Project
Percent for the Arts
City of Phoenix
Phoenix, AZ

Maui Embassy Suites Resort
Maui, HI
Interior Designers:
**Arthur Valdez &
Associates**
Newport Beach, CA

Coyote Cafe
Santa Fe, NM
Architect:
Studio Arquitectura
Santa Fe, NM

Salt River Project
Phoenix, AZ
Interior Designer:
**B. Eric Bron &
Associates**
Phoenix, AZ

James Sietz Residence
Santa Fe, NM
Architect:
Robert J. Strader, Jr., AIA
Santa Fe, NM

Slavin Residence
Brentwood, CA
Interior Designer:
**Frank K. Pennino &
Associates**
Los Angeles, CA

Publications

American Craft

Architectural Crafts, a Handbook

Artists of Taos

Contemporary Crafts for the Home

Designers West

Sunset

Southwest Art

Photo Credits

Craig Smith
Paul O'Connor

■ Dick Elliott

Dick Elliott
101 North Pearl
Ellensburg / Washington
98926

509.925.3224
509.925.5400 Fax

Innovative use of the reflector as a light-activated painting medium. Equally dynamic indoors or out, with natural or artificial light sources, when used in such diverse applications as murals, tunnels, parking garages, interior walls, building exteriors, columns, facades, and so on. Transforms encounters with ordinary surfaces into a truly dazzling experience that invites strong viewer interaction.

Patent pending on this unique process using reflectors. Video available upon request.

Selected Projects

Reflections on the Columbia
Reflectorized water tanks
City of Pateros
Pateros, WA

Cycle of the Sun
Henry Art Gallery
University of Washington
Seattle, WA

Sidewalk Designs
City of Ellensburg
Ellensburg, WA

Photo Credit
Richard Nicol
(top)

Awards

Bellevue Art Museum
Fellowship 1988
Bellevue, WA

Art Matters, Inc. 1989
New York City

Artist Trust GAP Grant 1989
Seattle, WA

■ Donna L. Dobberfuhl

Donna L. Dobberfuhl
Sculptural Designs
202 Fir Dale
Suite 104
Converse / Texas
78109

512.659.7250
800.397.1452 Toll Free

Clients Include

NCR Corporation

Silver Dollar City

University of Houston

Seminole Nation Museum

Southwestern Bell
Telephone

Arts Council
of Oklahoma City

Lutheran Church
Missouri Synod

Connecticut Commission
on the Arts

1

2

Selected Projects

1. *Mise-en-Scene*
10' x 100' sculpted brick
Johnson County
Community College
Theatre
Overland Park, KS

2. *Sisters II*
36" x 32" x 15"
outdoor bronze
Gardens of Art
Bellingham, WA

History of Duluth
6' x 75' sculpted brick
Canal Park
Public Arts Commission
Duluth, MN

*Andersonville POW
Memorial*
12' x 40' sculpted brick
6' courtyard bronze
American Ex-Prisoners
of War
Andersonville National
Historic Site
US National Park Service
Denver, CO

Con Carino
5 1/2' x 4' lobby bronze
Humana Women's &
Children's Hospital
San Antonio, TX

Accredited BFA sculptor
currently working with
brick and bronze in
conjunction with other
media. Work includes
realistic wildlife,
historical subjects,
contemporary people, and
expressionistic designs.

Member: National
Sculpture Society

Photo Credits

Bret A. Gustafson
Donna L. Dobberfuhl

■ Franz Mayer Mosaics

Franz Mayer of Munich, Inc.
Artistic Mosaics
Stained Glass
343 Passaic Avenue
Fairfield / New Jersey
07004

201.575.4777
201.575.5588 Fax

Established in 1845.
One of the leading
international studios
for artistic mosaics
and stained glass.

All work completed
in close collaboration
with the independent
artist / designer.

Offering full design,
execution, and
installation services.

Stained glass and
mosaics created for
thousands of public and
ecclesiastical buildings
around the world, many
of which have been
awarded landmark
status.

Selected Projects

Heart Tent
Artistic Glazing of Steel
Net Tent Construction
Diplomatic Club
Riyadh, Saudi Arabia
Artist / Architect:
Atelier Frei Otto

Freestyle
Ceramic Mural
Equitable Center
New York City
Artist:
Valerie Jaudon

Mosaic Triptych
1275 Pennsylvania Avenue
Washington, DC
Artist:
Miles Stafford Rolph

*The Tongue of the
Cherokee*
Glass Ceiling
Carnegie Museum of Art
Pittsburgh, PA
Artist:
Lothar Baumgarten

Roman 'Tethys' Mosaic
Harvard Business School
Morgan Hall
Boston
Restoration of Mosaic Floor
(probably largest ancient
mosaic in US)

■ M.C. CAROLYN

M.C. CAROLYN Sculptor &
Associates, Ltd.
316 Elm Avenue
Takoma Park / Maryland
20912

301.270.8094

Clients Include

University of Maryland
University College

National Museum of
Women in the Arts

Economic Development
Corporation

National Institute of
Health

Maryland-National Capitol
Park and Planning
Commission

The Thornton Collection
(Georgetown, KY)

Benedikt Wasmuth
(Munich, Germany)

St. Columba Catholic
Church
(Oxon Hill, MD)

Leonard A. Shapiro

David Evans

Exhibitions

University of Maryland
University College
College Park, MD 1990

Art in Public Places
Rockville, MD 1991

Chautauqua Art Assoc.
Chautauqua Institute
Chautauqua, NY 1991

The Hodson Gallery
Frederick, MD 1990-91

Hakone Open Air Museum
Tokyo, Japan 1988

John F. Kennedy Center
Washington, DC 1988

Wallace Wentworth
Gallery (solo exhibition)
Washington, DC 1985, 1986

Capital Children's Museum
Washington, DC 1987

Allied Artists of America
National Arts Club
New York City 1986

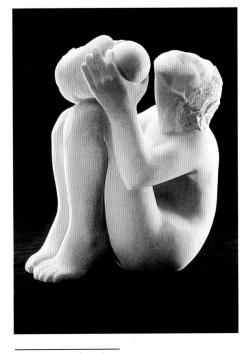

Unique benches, fountains,
and sculptures crafted
from stone and bronze by
an artist able to address
the technical requirements
of each site.

■ Joel A. Schwartz

Schwartz's Forge &
Metalworks, Inc.
PO Box 205
Forge Hollow Road
Deansboro / New York
13328

315.841.4477
315.841.4694 Fax

Design and production of
metalworks for interior
and exterior application,
created with sensitivity
toward environmental
design. All pieces are
produced with the skill
and tradition of the
blacksmith's art in mind,
with careful attention to
detail through all phases
of the project.

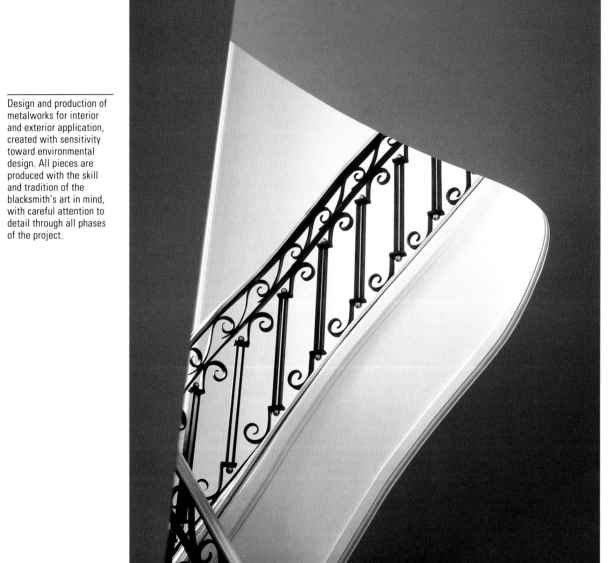

**Architectural Clients
Include**

**Boris Baranovich,
Architects**
New York City

**Centerbrook
Architects**
Essex, CT

**David Anthony
Easton Inc.**
New York City

**George Yu
Architects**
Philadelphia

**Jung / Brannen
Associates, Inc.**
Boston

**Mendel Mesick
Cohen Waite Hall,
Architects**
Albany, NY

**Robert A.M. Stern,
Architects**
New York City

**Tod Williams &
Associates**
New York City

New York Times

Commercial Renovation

Architectural Record

Builder

Architecture

■ Joel A. Schwartz / James R. Dean

Architectural Stairbuilding
& Handrailing
62 Pioneer Street
Cooperstown / New York
13326

607.547.2675
315.841.4477
315.841.4694 Fax

Selected Project

Private Residence
Alpine, NJ
Designer:
La Chenaire Designs
Alpine, NJ

Skilled craftsmen working together to provide coordinated design, fabrication, and installation of complex stairwork. These two independent artisans are a single source for high quality stairs, balustrades, and handrails.

■ Archwood, Inc.

Archwood, Inc.
2109 Great Trails Drive
Wooster / Ohio
44691

216.264.4563
800.545.1312 Toll Free
(in Ohio & surrounding states)
216.264.3935 Fax

Creating and restoring fine furniture and architectural pieces for public and private spaces.

Works primarily with architects and designers on projects for businesses, private homes, churches, temples and colleges.

Maintains close working relationships with stained glass artists, sculptors, metal fabricators, textile artisans and other craftspersons.

Established in 1981.

1

3

2

4

Selected Projects

1. Lectern (white oak)
First Presbyterian Church
Wooster, Ohio

2. Mirror
Neoclassical style
(mahogany)
Private Residence

3. Detail from dining table
Eastlake Victorian style
(walnut)
Private Residence

4. Restoration of 1901
Knabe grand piano
(rosewood)
Private Residence

Photo Credit
Tony Festa
Photography

Specialties Include

Fine Furniture

Architectural Woodwork

Conservation &
Restoration

■ John Luttmann

Luttmann Brothers
Woodcarving & Sign
Company
15 South Main Street
Phoenixville / Pennsylvania
19460

215.935.0920
215.933.9205 Fax

Selected Projects

ARCO Chemical Company
Headquarters
Newtown Square, PA

Stoneridge Corporate
Center
Exton, PA

The Vanguard Group
Valley Forge, PA

Zoo Atlanta
Atlanta, GA

Hotel Cheyanne
Euro Disneyland
France

Mikasa...Lifestyles
Secaucus, NJ

Tiger Stop
National Zoological Park
Washington, DC

Signage, architectural
ornamentation, and point
of purchase displays.

Design through fabrication
of contemporary,
traditional, and historical
signage. Ornamentation
with an emphasis on relief
and sculptural carving.

Large-scale dimensional
pieces that integrate
signage and sculpture,
fabricated from Sign-Foam
(a rigid polyurethane
foam, available in sheet
and block stock).

In-house mold making
capability and casting
facilities to meet quantity
requirements.

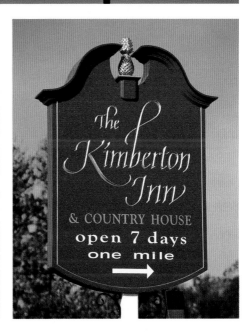

■ Nick Strange

The Century Guild
PO Box 13128
Research Triangle Park /
North Carolina
27709

919.598.1612

Builders of one-of-a-kind
furniture or architectural
elements for corporate,
ecclesiastical, and
residential settings.
Specializing in solid
hardwoods and veneers,
in traditional and
contemporary styles.

Other Projects Include

Boardroom Furniture
Glaxo Inc.
Research Triangle Park, NC
Architect:
O'Brien / Atkins
Research Triangle Park, NC

William R. Kenan, Jr. Fund
Chapel Hill, NC
Architect:
O'Brien / Atkins
Research Triangle Park, NC

Residential Furniture
Private Residence
Hilton Head, SC
Architect:
Meyer-Greeson
Charlotte, NC

Statue Base
Our Lady of Fifth Avenue
St. Thomas Church
New York City
Architect:
Bennett-Wallace
New York City

Altar
Trinity Episcopal Church
Milton, CT
Designer:
Terry Byrd Eason
Chapel Hill, NC

Architectural Woodwork
Ayr Mount (built 1813-17)
Residence of Richard H.
Jenrette
Hillsborough, NC

Selected Project

Columbarium Cabinets
St. Thomas Church
New York City
Architect:
**Allen, Harbinson &
Associates**
New York City

Photo Credit
Richard Faughn

■ Randy Cochran

Wood Studio
Route 3 Box 427
Decatur / Alabama
35603

205.350.5270

One-of-a-kind, limited production, and site specific woodwork, including tables, chairs, and cabinets. Wood with leather, stone, metal, glass, and synthetics.

Specializing in small- to medium-scale projects requiring personal attention.

Collaborative work welcome.

Selected Projects

1. Cherry armoire
Colonial Williamsburg
Foundation
Williamsburg, VA
In Collaboration With:
**Williamsburg Inn
Design Studio**
Williamsburg, VA

2. Rocking chair
(oak and leather)
Private Collection

3. Ash table
Children's Hospital
Birmingham, AL
In Collaboration With:
Hatcher Design
Birmingham, AL

4. Executive furniture
(mahogany and marble)
20th Century Marketing
Huntsville, AL
In Collaboration With:
Adams Design
Honolulu

■ May Bender

May Bender Design
Associates
7 Deer Park Drive
Princeton Corporate Plaza
Monmouth Junction /
New Jersey
08852

908.329.8388
908.329.0612 Fax

Market-oriented design firm, specializing in industrial design, packaging and product design, and corporate identity (including interior design) for over 35 years, with current emphasis on the fine arts.

Original artworks include oil paintings, pen and ink drawings, and watercolors.

Appropriate for corporate and residential spaces. Sizes range from small to over six feet.

Commissioned artwork of any size will be considered. Completed paintings are available for immediate hanging.

Clients Include

Becton Dickson & Co.

Celanese, Inc.

Cheseborough Pond's Inc.

Cosmetic Surgery Center of Connecticut

Estee Lauder, Inc.

The Gillette Company

International Gold Corporation, Ltd.

Johnson & Johnson

Harold Kent, AIA

Lever Bros., Co.

Lorillard, Inc.

Old London (Division of Borden, Inc.)

Revlon, Inc.

RJ Reynolds, Inc.

Schering Plough Corporation

Sterling Drug, Inc.

United Presbyterian Church

Wear-Ever/
Proctor-Silex, Inc.

Warner Lambert Company

Awards

Package Design Council International's *Packaging Person of the Year* 1985

CLIO
New York City 1980

Les Seymour / Brenda Seymour

Envirographics
2325 Third Street
Studio 347
San Francisco / California
94107

415.861.1118
415.861.0326 Fax

Artists specializing in the design, execution, and installation of hand-painted murals, folding screens, and painted tapestries.

Custom fine art available in a wide range of styles, from Classical to Modern Realism. Even very large murals exceeding 2000 square feet are created in the San Francisco studios on canvas.

1

Selected Projects

1. Lobby Mural
Hotel Villa Florence
San Francisco

2. Folding Screen (detail)
Private Collection
9' high x 16' wide

3. Restaurant Mural
(detail)
Grand Hyatt Wailea
Maui, HI

4. Painted Tapestry
(detail)
Greyhound / Dial
Corporate Center
Phoenix

2

3

4

■ Ellsworth Perriwinkle, Ltd.

Robert E. Cox
Ellen Graham
1323 Hollins Street
Baltimore / Maryland
21223

410.685.6912

Services Include

Surface Design
Consultation

Trompe L'Oeil, Mural,
and Detailing Design

Faux Finish
(all materials)

Deviated Surface
Treatments

Decorative painting and
surface design,
specializing in traditional
and innovative glazing,
metallic gilding, and
deviated surface
treatments for commercial
and significant residential
projects worldwide.

Photo Credit
Don Carstens

■ Modeworks

54 Leonard Street
New York / New York
10013

212.226.4079
212.226.9258 Fax

Columbus / Ohio
614.297.6844

Dallas / Texas
214.426.1334

Working with architects
and designers to create
artwork for retail,
corporate and residential
clientele.

Vitalizing the environment
and enhancing surfaces
with painted illusions,
finishes and murals.

Constructing three
dimensional props and
displays with artistic
originality.

Clients Include

1. Kookai, Inc.
Paris, France

2. Limited Express

Beyer, Blinder Belle

Skidmore, Owings & Merril

Arnel Bickford Marketing

The Limited Inc

Scottish Rite Childrens
Hospital

Cato-Gobe and Associates

Hard Rock

Ashley Bickerton

Metropolitan Home

George Hamilton Residence

Stanley Felderman &
Associates

Haseko Inc

■ Modeworks Conservation

54 Leonard Street
New York / New York
10013

212.226.4079
212.226.9258 Fax

Columbus / Ohio
614.297.6844

Dallas / Texas
214.426.1334

Experts on historic
preservation and
conservation of major
monuments, mural
paintings and objects of
fine art, executed for
public agencies, museums
and private clients.
Consultation for historic
preservation, and
execution of decorative
painting.

1

Clients Include

1. Superintendent of Fine Art
Salerno, Italy

2. Justin Management
New York City

Department of Parks &
Recreation
New York City

Superintendent of Fine Art
Florence, Italy

The Wolfsonian
Foundation

Sotheby, Inc.

Safani Gallery

Monastery Certosa Di
Padula National Museum
Italy

Superintendent of Fine Art
Berlin, Germany

The Plaster Museum
Pietrasanta, Italy

2

■ Conrad Schmitt Studios

Conrad Schmitt Studios
2405 South 162nd Street
New Berlin / Wisconsin
53151

414.786.3030
800.969.3033 Toll Free
414.786.9036 Fax

Established in 1889.
Experienced in the
conservation of the
traditional, as well as
the creation of the
contemporary. Involved in
the preservation and
renovation of numerous
structures of architectural
and historic significance
across the country.
Whether working directly
with the client or through
the architect or designer,
the studio is an effective
part of the team,
achieving excellence
through the quality of
its art.

1

Selected Projects

1. Wang Center for the
Performing Arts
Boston
Architect:
**Notter Finegold &
Alexander**
Boston

Federal Building,
U.S. Courthouse
Milwaukee, WI
Client:
**General Services
Administration**
Chicago

University of Notre Dame
Sacred Heart Church
South Bend, IN
Architect:
Ellerbe Becket Company
Minneapolis, MN

Union Station
St. Louis, MO
Architect:
**Hellmuth, Obata &
Kassabaum**
St. Louis, MO

Waldorf-Astoria Hotel
New York City
Architect:
**Kenneth E. Hurd &
Associates**
Boston

Photo Credit
Copyright 1990
Roger Farrington

■ **Glass**

■ Larry Zgoda

Larry Zgoda Stained Glass
3447 North Pulaski Road
Chicago / Illinois
60641

312.463.1874

Publications

Contemporary Crafts for
the Home

Matter

Home

Professional Stained
Glass

American Craft

Stained Glass Quarterly

Glass Art

Designs and fabricates
timeless, original
compositions in stained,
leaded glass. Works are in
residential, corporate, and
liturgical environments,
and public places.
Compositions embrace
architectonic, decorative,
and symbolic genres and
are appropriate for many
transparent and
translucent applications.
Doorlights, skylights,
transoms, sidelights,
cabinet doors, and
clerestories are some of
the usual applications. Has
a thorough knowledge of
the craft and a confident
grasp of design. Creative
handling of materials and
intuitive approach to
composition have produced
works that satisfy the most
demanding conditions.

Photo Credit
Christopher Kean

■ Deanne Sabeck

Deanne Sabeck
Studio 215
710 13th Street
San Diego / California
92101

619.234.0814

1

Artist and designer exploring the contradictory properties of glass, light, stone, and metal. Creating site-specific installations that capture both the spirit of the architecture and the functional aspect of the building.

Applications for both corporate and residential clients include entryways, windows, wall sculpture, free-standing sculpture, and furniture.

Recipient: Merit Award in Architectural Glass, American Crafts Awards, 1991.

Selected Projects

Morris Udahl Recreation Center
1. Interior view
2. Exterior view
Glass and copper entryway wall
14'w x 20'h
Tucson, AZ
Architect:
Brooks & Associates
Tucson, AZ

Hotel Westcourt
Curved glass wall
8'w x 32'h
Phoenix
Architect:
Allen & Philip Architects
Phoenix

The Boulders Resort
Two skylights
Carefree, AZ
Architect:
Bob Bacon, AIA
Carefree, AZ

Private Residence
Entryway
Rancho Santa Fe, CA
Interior Designer:
Paul Shotz
San Diego, CA

Private Residence
Wall sculpture
6'w x 6'h
Austin, TX

2

Photo Credit
Robin Stancliff

■ Pacific Art Glass

Pacific Art Glass
1200 College Walk
Suite 107
Honolulu / Hawaii
96817

808.537.3758
808.526.0736 Fax

Other Clients Include

Hilton Corporation

Stark Ventures Ltd.

Mauna Lani Bay Resort

Toyota Motor Corporation

Bank of Hawaii

Royal Hawaiian Hotel

State of Hawaii

EEC Industries
(Canada)

Guam Hyatt Hotel

Matura Beach Resort
(Malaysia)

Mauna Kea Hotel

Obayashi Group

Architectural Clients Include

Media Five
Honolulu
Australia

Gulstrom • Kosko Group
Honolulu

Leo A. Daly
Honolulu

Concept Design Group
Honolulu
Singapore

Lacayo Architects
Honolulu

AM Partners
Honolulu

Wimberly, Allison, Tong & Goo, Inc.
Honolulu

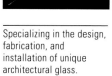
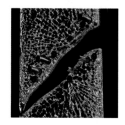

Specializing in the design, fabrication, and installation of unique architectural glass.

Photo Credits
Ed Espero
David Franzen

■ Frank Close

Frank Close
397 West Twelfth Street
New York / New York
10014

212.989.7039
212.807.8950 Fax

In collaboration with the architect, designer, and client, distinctive architectural glassworks are created using the unique color and refracting properties of blown, cut, bevelled, and etched glass.

Site-specific installations respond to surroundings, informed by quality of light, use of space, psychological environment, and architectural style.

Architectural Clients Include

Shepley Bulfinch Richardson & Abbott
Boston

RTKL Associates, Inc.
Baltimore

Tony Chi & Associates
New York City

Walz Design
New York City

Grad Associates
Newark, NJ

Guyon / Walton Inc.
Lexington, KY

Tom Lee Ltd.
New York City

Other Clients Include

IBM

Prudential Insurance Company

Phillips Academy (Andover,. MA)

Costain Group

Doral Country Club

Liberty National Bank

Pace University

Photo Credit
Walt Roycraft

Merridy Pohlmann & Jed Palmer

Palmer-Pohlmann
Studio, Inc.
5344 B Peachtree Road
Chamblee / Georgia
30341

404.454.9767
800.854.7528 Toll Free
404.455.6020 Fax

Incorporating art as an integral part of the architecture to create site-specific glassworks. A full spectrum of styles is available, including leaded, sandblasted, or sculptural glass. Finished products include one-of-a-kind sculptures and awards as well as leaded and stained glass panels.

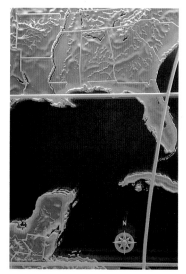

Services

Design Consulting

CADD

Beveling

Laminating

Sandblasting:
etching
3-dimensional carving
CADD-pattern etching

Special Textures:
gluechipping
granite
marble veining

Installation

Publications

Glass Art Magazine

Southern Occasions

Atlanta Journal

Professional Stained Glass

Business Atlanta

■ Jed Wallach / Chris Wallach

The Wallach Glass Studio
1580 Sebastopol Road
Santa Rosa / California
95407

707.527.1205
707.573.1493 Fax

Designers and creators of etched glass, deep carved glass, architectural stained glass, lighting fixtures, signage, and floor and wall systems. Innovative techniques include three-dimensional carving in thick sheets of German waterwhite crystal, V-cut lettering for enhanced readability of graphics, metal and other inlays, and special framing and lighting.

Architectural Clients Include

Gensler & Associates
Los Angeles
San Francisco

Studios
San Francisco

Leo A. Daly
Los Angeles
San Francisco

Kaplan McLaughlin Diaz
San Francisco

Charles Pfister
San Francisco

Robinson Mills & Williams
San Francisco

Simon Martin-Vegue Winkelstein Moris
San Francisco

BOOR/A Architects
Portland

Publications

Architectural Record

Progressive Architecture

Interior Design

Designer's West

Hotel & Restaurant Design

Photo Credit
John Sutton

■ J. Gorsuch Collins

J. Gorsuch Collins
8283 West Iliff Lane
Lakewood / Colorado
80227

303.985.8081
303.980.0692 Fax

Specializing in works that exude originality and compatibility with the architectural setting, designed in collaboration with the architect.

Works incorporate a wide variety of techniques, often in combination with other materials or with other artists, providing interesting departures from previous works.

Custom blown, etched, fused, and beveled glass allow maximum versatility in texture. Smaller architectural accessories that complement the main installation are also available.

Delivery and installation possible both nationally and internationally.

Selected Projects

Zenith Restaurant
Denver, CO
Architect:
Gensler Architects
Denver, CO

Colorado Legislative
Services Building
Denver, CO
1% for the Arts Project

Littleton Hospital Chapel
Littleton, CO
Architect:
Davis Partnership
Denver, CO

Kaiser Permanente
Denver, CO
Architect:
Klipp Partnership
Denver, CO

St. Anne's Episcopal School
Denver, CO
Architect:
**Murato Outland
Architects**
Denver, CO

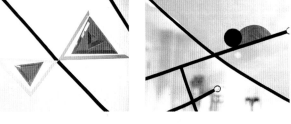

Photo Credits
Hedrich Blessing
Kosloff Photography

■ Joel Berman

Joel Berman Glass
Studios, Ltd.
1-1244 Cartwright Street
Granville Island
Vancouver /
British Columbia
Canada V6H 3R8

604.684.8332
604.684.8373 Fax

Clients Include

Canadian Airlines
International

Canadian National
Railways

Towers Perrin

Four Seasons Hotel
(Vancouver)

Cathedral Place

Ferguson Gifford

Marine Building
(Vancouver)

Russell Du Moulin

Thompson Dorfman
Sweatman

Canadian Imperial Bank of
Commerce

Selected Projects

1. *Suspension*
Cable-hung, colored,
curved, and laminated
glass collage featuring
antique glass with
dichroic glass appliqué
Domestic Empress Lounge
Lester B. Pearson
International Airport
Toronto
Interior Design:
City Interiors Ltd.
Vancouver, BC (Canada)
and **BBA Design
Consultants**
Vancouver, BC (Canada)

2. Autonomous Collage
Colored, laminated glass
Towers Perrin
Vancouver, BC (Canada)
Interior Designer:
**Group 5 Design
Associates**
Vancouver, BC (Canada)

Specializing in the design
and fabrication of
successful architectural
glass art for commercial
interior space, with
emphasis on corporate
offices and building lobbies.
Work includes most forms
of flat, bent, and etched
glass as well as indoor and
outdoor glass sculpture.

■ Lilliana

Lilliana
1250 Long Beach Avenue
Los Angeles / California
90021

213.627.8231
213.622.1712 Fax

Watertown /
Massachusetts
617.926.3684
617.926.8183 Fax

Contemporary fused
glass designs that
incorporate custom
inlaying techniques.

Projects include interior
and exterior tile
applications, glass
relief, and backlit
environments that
maximize the effects of
light within a full color
range.

Architectural
installations range from
simple windows,
fireplaces, swimming
pools, doors, counters,
and cabinets to entire
glass wall murals.

Clients Include

Ciasco Residence

de Escobar Residence

Stein Residence

Gorman Residence

Groton Community School

Rossinow Residence

Dr. Sylvio P. Lessa

Neumann Residence

Century Auto

Miller Residence

Masciale Designs

Lewis Residence

Chodin Residence

Aceto Residence

Santilli Residence

Grodman Residence

Dr. Deciode Escobar

Dr. Peter Nair

Good Samaritan Hospital

Dr. JoAnne Fineman

Photo Credit

James Creighton

■ Ellen Mandelbaum

Ellen Mandelbaum
Glass Art
39-49 46th Street
Sunnyside Gardens
New York / New York
11104

718.361.8154
718.361.8154 Fax

Specializing in painted and leaded glass panels that complement architectural detailing or help improve views. Panels can be built in or suspended over existing light sources.

Works featured in international exhibitions and created in collaboration with architects, interior designers, and clients to create light and beautiful spaces.

Painted glass fired at 1200° for permanence Handmade painted or silk-screened sheet glass can be custom made for special projects.

Reliable service since 1981.

Selected Projects

1. Hanging panels for bay window
Lusterman Residence
Baldwin, Long Island, NY

Square arch for reception area
Recording Studio
Architect:
Wasserman & Waterhouse
New York City

Hall doors
Residence of Adina Taylor
Architect:
Adina Taylor, AIA
New York CIty

Large hall window
Seiler Residence
Duluth, MN

Light screen for privacy
Country Home
Interior Designer:
Ray Bennett
New York City

■ Architectural Glass Art, Inc.

Kenneth F. vonRoenn,
President
Tim O'Neill, Vice President
PO Box 4665
1110 Baxter Avenue
Louisville / Kentucky
40204

502.585.5421
502.585.2808 Fax

A unique glass studio that develops new techniques to expand the potential and application of glass as a contemporary architectural art.

Fabricates the work of leading independent glass artists, thereby offering alternatives to clients in selecting the most appropriate individual for the design of their project.

Provides clients with the highest level of professionalism and quality.

Selected Projects

Mountain View City Hall
Mountain View, CA
Architect:
**William Turnbull &
Associates**
San Francisco

University of Oregon
Eugene, OR
Architect:
Charles Moore
Los Angeles

Yale University
Battell Chapel
Architect:
**Herman Newman &
Associates**
New Haven, CT

Gerald Hines Residence
Aspen, CO
Architects:
Charles Moore
Los Angeles and
William Turnbull
San Francisco

St. Louis International
Airport
Architect:
Christner Partnership
St. Louis

J. Pierpont Morgan Library
New York City
Architect:
Voorsanger & Mills
New York City

Publications

AIA Journal

Progressive Architecture

Metropolitan Home

Architectural Digest

Interior Design

American Craft

Architecture

Interior

Residential Interiors

Realities

Jean-Jacques Duval

Duval Studio
Gypsy Trail
Carmel / New York
10512

914.225.6077

Represented by
Rohlf's Studio, Inc.
914.699.4848

Specializing in faceted, leaded, and stained glass windows for religious, commercial, residential, or corporate applications.

Photo Credit
Julius Schulman

Selected Projects

B'nai Zion
El Paso, TX
Architect:
Sidney Eisenshtat
Beverly Hills, CA

Beth El Synagogue
Minneapolis, MN
Architect:
Bertram L. Bassuk
New York City

Temple Israel
Boston
Architect:
The Architects Collaborative
Cambridge, MA

B'nai Jeshurun
Short Hills, NJ
Architect:
Belluschi, Gruzen & Partners
Portland, OR
New York City

Pennsylvania State University
Altoona, PA
Architect:
Campbell Rea Hayes & Large
Altoona, PA

Kasugai Seibu Center
Nagoya, Japan
Architect:
Yendo Associates
Tokyo, Japan

■ Wilmark Studios

Wilmark Studios Inc.
177 South Main Street
Pearl River / New York
10965

914.735.7443

Clients Include

Albinas Elskus

Willy Malarcher

Ellen Mandlebaum

Yaraslava Mills

Brigitte Pasternak

Robert Pinart

Hendrik Vandeburgt

Efram Weitzman

Paul Wood

Photo Credit
Mark Liebowitz

Fabrication and
installation of leaded and
stained glass windows
employing various surface
treatments in a
collaborative process with
artist, architect, designer,
and clients.

Selected Projects

The National Arts Club
New York City
two skylight windows
Designer:
Albinas Elskus
New York City

St. Vincent Hospital Chapel
New York City
restoration & new stained
glass windows
Designer:
Hendrik Vandeburgt
Westwood, NJ

St. Luke's Church
Long Beach, CA
stained glass transoms
Designer:
Robert Pinart
Nyack, NJ

Sacred Heart Church
Cambria Heights, NY
ten stained glass windows
Designer:
Willy Malarcher
Englewood, NJ

National Cathedral
Washington, DC
four chapel windows
Designer:
Robert Pinart
Nyack, NY

■ Rohlf's Studio, Inc.

Peter A. Rohlf
Peter H. Rohlf
783 South Third Avenue
Mt. Vernon / New York
10550

914.699.4848
212.823.4545
212.823.4717 Fax

Collaborating on an international level to achieve the highest degree of integrity between art and architecture.

Creating and working in all mediums of leaded, stained, faceted, laminated, beveled, etched, and dimensional glass for liturgical and commercial commissions.

Architectural Clients Include

Hardy Holzman Pfieffer
New York City

Beyer, Blinder, Belle
New York City

Yendo Associates
New York
Tokyo

Peter L. Gluck & Partners
New York City

James Stewart Polshek & Partners
New York City

Shope Reno Warton Associates
Greenwich, CT

Kevin Roche John Dinkeloo & Associates, Inc.
Hamden, CT

Photo Credit
Steve Ostrow

Selected Project

Ferncliff Mausoleum
Hartsdale, NY
Architect:
Joseph J. Mangan, AIA
Hohokus, NJ

■ David Wilson

David Wilson Design
RD2 Box 121A
South New Berlin /
New York
13843

607.334.3015
607.334.7065 Fax

Designs, fabricates and
installs projects that
integrate art with
architecture.

Selected Projects

Corporate Boardroom,
Corning, Inc.
New York City
Architect:
**Kevin Roche John
Dinkeloo and Associates**
Hamden, CT

Ives Public Library
New Haven, CT
Architect:
**Hardy, Holzman, Pfeiffer
Associates**
New York City

St. Paul's Catholic Church
Tampa, FL
Architect:
The Ashford Group
Clearwater, FL

  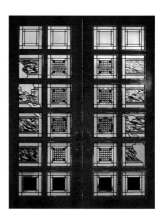

Photo Credit
Richard Walker

Index

Alphabetical / State / Discipline Index

State / Discipline / Alphabetical Index

James Edwards	MA	IR	25
James Edwards, Illustration	MA	IR	25
Einer Model Company	TX	MM	107
Dick Elliott	WA	FAA	206
Ray Elliott Associates	GA	IR	66
Ellsworth Perriwinkle, Ltd.	MD	FAA	220
Enamels by Kay Whitcomb	MA	FAA	194
Envirographics	CA	FAA	219
Environmental Sculpture	PA	FAA	193
Bill Evans	WA	IR	63
Exhibitgroup	TX	MM	120
N.H. Fedder Associates, Inc.	NY	LD	96
Rob Fisher	PA	FAA	193
Dudley Fleming	OH	IR	69
David Floyd	FL	FAA	200
David Floyd Sculpture	FL	FAA	200
Stephen H. Ford	MD	MM	117
Franzen Photography	HI	AP	146
David Franzen	HI	AP	146
Rob Fraser	NY	AP	153
Steve Fritz	MI	IR	71
Steve Fritz Art Service	MI	IR	71
Genesis Studios	FL, MA	IR	28-29
Charles F. Giles	HI	IR	61
Charles F. Giles, Illustrator	HI	IR	61
John Gillan	FL	AP	168
John Gillan Photography, Inc.	FL	AP	168
Ellen Graham	MD	FAA	220
Anton Grassl	MA	AP	133
Sam Gray	MA	AP	136
Sam Gray Photography	MA	AP	136
George Greenamyer	MA	FAA	189
Gordon Grice	ON (Canada)	IR	53
Gordon Grice & Associates	ON (Canada)	IR	53
Philip Grussenmeyer	IL	AP	165
Dan Ham	NM, TX	AP	169
Dan Ham Photography	TX	AP	169
Dan Harmon	GA	IR	32
Dan Harmon & Associates	GA	IR	32
HELIOSTUDIO	MN, NY	AP	183
William Hemmerdinger	CA	SPEC	104
Carl Hillmann Associates Lighting Design, Inc.	NY	LD	89
Gary Hofheimer	HI	AP	180